LEXICON LABS TIT
STEM
Python for Teens: A Step-by-
QUANTUM COMPUTING for Smart Pre-Te
PHYSICS NERD: 1000+ Amazing And Mind-
BIOLOGY NERD: 1000+ Amazing And Mind-
CHEMISTRY NERD: 1000+ Amazing And Mind
ASTRONOMY NERD: 1000+ Amazing And Mind-Blowing ruc..
AI for Smart Kids Ages 6-9: Discover How Artificial Intelligence is Changing the ...
Code Breakers: A Practical Guide to Mastering Programming Languages and Algorithms
Quantum Nerd Quizmaster Edition: Quantum Quizzes that Educate, Entertain and Challenge
The AI Nerd: Quizmaster Edition Mind-Blowing AI Quizzes that Educate, Entertain and Challenge
AI for Smart Pre-Teens and Teens Ages 10-19: Using Artificial Intelligence to Learn, Think, and Create
CHEMISTRY NERD BOOK II: 1000+ More Amazing and Mind-Blowing Facts About Chemistry
(Spanish Translation) LA IA ESTÁ AQUÍ: Usa la Inteligencia Artificial para Aprender, Pensar y Crear

ENTREPRENEURSHIP
10 Life Hacks Every Teen Should Know
Innovation Handbook for Teen Entrepreneurs
Teen Innovators: 30 Teen Trailblazers and their Breakthrough Ideas

GREAT SCIENTISTS SERIES
Nikola Tesla: An Electrifying Genius
John von Neumann: The Giga Brain
Einstein: The Man, The Myth, The Legend
Newton: Genius of the Scientific Revolution
Darwin: Unlocking the Secrets of Evolution
Richard Feynman: The Adventures of a Curious Physicist
Marie Curie: Unleashing Radioactivity for Human Progress

GREAT INNOVATORS SERIES
Elon: A Modern Renaissance Man
Steve Jobs: The Visionary Innovator of Silicon Valley
Walt Disney: Creator of an Entertainment Empire

GREAT LEADERS SERIES
Cleopatra: Queen of the Nile
Gandhi: Freedom Fighter and Global Icon
MLK Jr: A Dream Deferred, A Legacy Defined
Ben Franklin: Innovator, Statesman, Visionary
Churchill: The Spirit of an Indomitable Leader
Lincoln: Emancipator and Defender of the Union
Jimmy Carter: A Century of Integrity and Service
St. Francis of Assisi: The Humble Servant of God
George Washington: The First American President
Alexander the Great: Conqueror, Visionary, Legend
Nelson Mandela: Visionary Freedom Fighter and Statesman
Mark Antony: The Rise and Tragic Fall of a Roman Legend
Jefferson: Statesman, Visionary and the Third US President
Julius Caesar: The Rise and Fall of Rome's Greatest Leader
St. Ignatius of Loyola: Revolutionizing Faith and Education

GREAT EXPLORERS SERIES
Lewis and Clark: Blazing a Trail to the West
Magellan: First Circumnavigator of the Earth
Shackleton: Pioneering Explorer of the Antarctic
Columbus: The Explorer who Changed the World
Robert Falcon Scott: A Pioneer of Antarctic Exploration

Marco Polo: Intrepid Explorer who Bridged East and West
Captain Cook: The Legendary Seafarer, Navigator, and Explorer

GREAT ARTISTS SERIES
Taylor Swift: The Ascent of a Superstar
Andy Warhol: The Pop Art Phenomenon
Van Gogh: Troubled Soul and Visionary Artist
Claude Monet: The Master of Impressionism
Michelangelo: Enigmatic Artist, Enigmatic Genius
Frida Kahlo: Unbroken Spirit: Artist, Activist, and Icon

TRIVIAL PURSUITS
Coffee Secrets
Vanishing Sun
Nobel Laureates 2023
Nobel Laureates 2024
Philosophy Brain-Teasers
Devilish Puzzles for Smart Kids
20th Century Wordsearch Extravaganza

COLORING BOOKS
Spaced Out
Vintage Auto
Orchid Fever
Serenity Now
Concept Cars
Mermaid Magic
Stoner Paradise
Swear.Laugh.Color.
Impossible Espresso
Perfectly Square Zen
Rebels of the Outback
Style with Confidence
Fantastical Creatures
Fabulous Fashionistas
National Parks Canada
101 Flower Arrangements
African Safari: A Mindfulness Coloring Book
Beautiful Australia: A Mindfulness Coloring Book
Magnificent South America: A Mindfulness Coloring Book
National Parks: Great Landscapes from America's Top National Parks

PLANT GENIUS

The Science and Secrets of Plant Intelligence

© 2025 by Dr. Leo Lexicon

Notice of Rights

All rights reserved. No portion of this publication may be reproduced, distributed, or transmitted in any form or by any means, electronic or mechanical, including photocopying, recording, or any information storage and retrieval system, without prior written permission from the author. Reproduction or translation of this work in any form beyond that permitted by Sections 107 or 108 of the 1976 United States Copyright Act is strictly prohibited. No companion books, summaries, or study guides are authorized under this notice. For other permission requests, please contact the author.

Liability Disclaimer

The information provided within this book is for general informational purposes only. While every effort has been made to keep the information up-to-date and correct, there are no representations or warranties, express or implied, about the completeness, accuracy, reliability, suitability, or availability with respect to the information, products, services, or related graphics contained in this book for any purpose. Any use of this information is at your own risk. All images in this publication were originally conceptualized and generated by the author, who holds the copyright.

The author, company, and publisher shall in no event be held liable for any loss or other damages, including but not limited to special, incidental, consequential, or other damages. This disclaimer applies to any damages caused by any failure of performance, error, omission, interruption, deletion, delay in transmission or transmission, defect, computer malware, communication line failure, theft, destruction, or unauthorized access to or use of records, whether for breach of contract, tort, negligence, or under any other cause of action.

By reading this book, you agree to use the contents entirely at your own risk and that you are solely responsible for your use of the contents. The author, company, and publisher do not warrant the performance or applicability of any references listed in this book. All references and links are for informational purposes only and are not warranted for content, accuracy, or any other implied or explicit purpose.

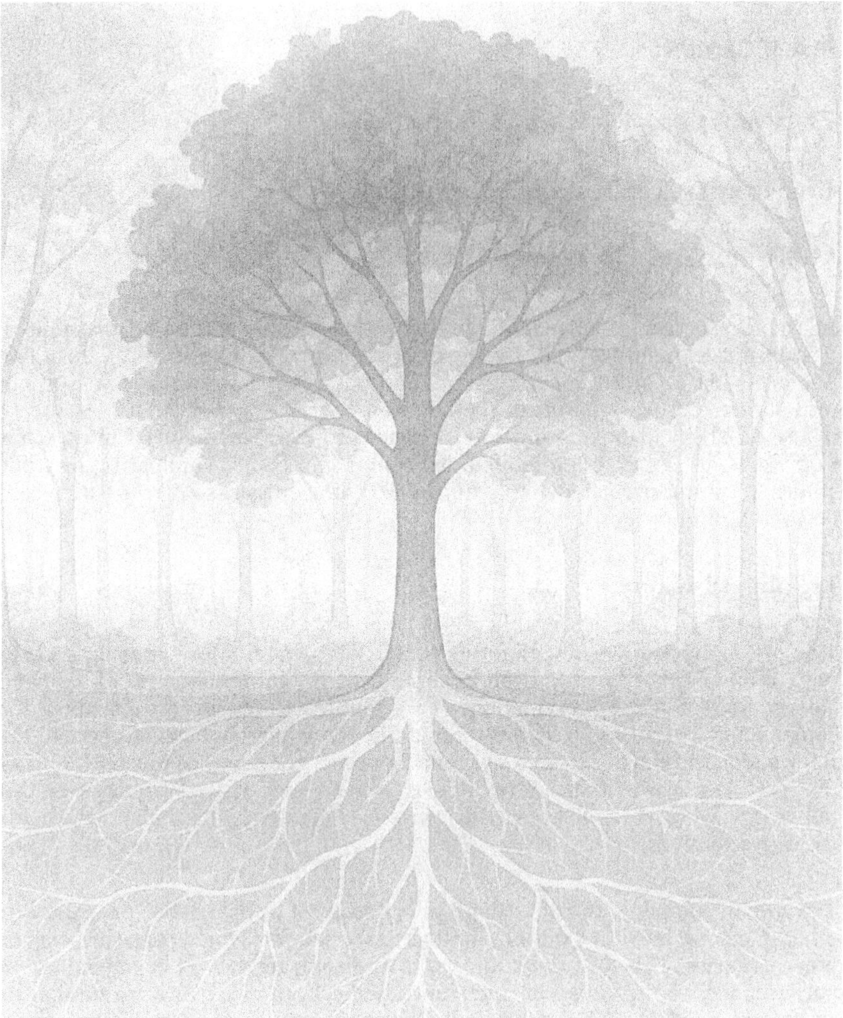

PLANT GENIUS

The Science and Secrets of Plant Intelligence

by

Dr. Leo Lexicon

PLANT GENIUS

The Science and Secrets of Plant Intelligence

Have you ever wondered how plants know when to grow, when to bloom, or even when to warn their neighbors of danger? While we often think of plants as still and silent, they are actually incredibly active, intelligent, and deeply connected to one another. This book is your guide to discovering the hidden world of plant communication—one that has been unfolding in the soil beneath our feet for millions of years.

From the smallest root to the tallest tree, plants are part of a vast, invisible network that allows them to share resources, send warnings, and even support one another in times of need. This network, known as the "Wood Wide Web," is made up of mycorrhizal fungi that link plants together underground, forming a kind of biological internet. These fungi help plants exchange nutrients, water, and chemical signals, creating a cooperative system that supports entire forests.

But it doesn't stop there. Plants also use smells, sounds, and vibrations to communicate with each other and with the world around them. Some release chemicals into the air to alert others of threats, while others respond to music, wind, and even touch. They can remember past experiences, adapt to changing conditions, and even work together to survive.

This book takes you on an exciting journey through the science of plant life, exploring how they interact, how they learn, and how they shape the world around them. You will discover:

- How trees talk to one another through fungal networks

- Why some plants smell like flowers and others like garlic

- How plants "hear" and "feel" their environment

- What it means for plants to be smart, even without a brain

- How this knowledge can help us grow better food, protect ecosystems, and build a more sustainable future

Whether you are a curious student, a nature lover, or simply someone who wants to understand the world in a new way, *The Genius of Plants* will open your eyes to the amazing intelligence and resilience of the green world around you. You will rethink what it means to be alive, and learn how we can live more harmoniously with the natural world.

At the end of each chapter in this book, readers will find a special section titled "Did You Know?" that highlights surprising or amusing *fun facts* about plant intelligence that reveal just how unexpectedly clever, responsive, and socially aware plants can be. In addition, the book includes a Classroom Activities section packed with discussion questions and experiment ideas, making it an ideal resource for science teachers and students exploring plant biology, ecology, or environmental science. To support comprehension and encourage deeper learning, the book also features a Glossary of Technical Terms, a Timeline of Important Discoveries, and a brief list of References for further study. This book is not designed to be a passive reading experience. Rather, it is an interactive, inquiry-driven learning tool that will enable you to appreciate the wonders of this important field.

So, are you ready to uncover the secret language of plants and see the world in a whole new way? Let us begin.

Dr. Leo Lexicon is an educator and author. He is the founder of Lexicon Labs, a publishing imprint that is focused on creating entertaining books for active minds.

CONTENTS

CHAPTER 1 1
MYCORRHIZAL FUNGI: THE INVISIBLE NETWORK 1
- INTRODUCTION 1
- THE WORLD BENEATH OUR FEET 2
- THE WOOD WIDE WEB 5
- COMMUNICATION THROUGH THE FUNGAL NETWORK 8
- WHY THIS MATTERS? 10
- DID YOU KNOW? 12

CHAPTER 2 13
THE LANGUAGE OF SMELLS 13
- PLANT COMMUNICATION 13
- THE ROLE OF VOCS 15
- VOLATILE COMPOUNDS AND PLANT DEFENSE 18
- ROOT EXUDATES: SIGNALS BENEATH THE SOIL 21
- ATTRACTING ALLIES: PHEROMONES AND POLLINATION 23
- KEEPING PESTS AT BAY 25
- DID YOU KNOW? 27

CHAPTER 3 29
THE SCIENCE OF PLANT SENSITIVITY 29
- PLANTS ARE SUPER-SENSORS 29
- SOUND AND PLANT GROWTH 32
- ROOTS AND VIBRATION 35
- THE MYSTERY OF PLANT PERCEPTION 37
- DID YOU KNOW? 39

CHAPTER 4 40
THE SOCIAL LIVES OF PLANTS 40
- COOPERATION AND SUPPORT 40
- THE STRUGGLE FOR SURVIVAL 44
- MEMORY AND LEARNING IN PLANTS 46
- INTELLIGENCE WITHOUT A BRAIN 49
- DID YOU KNOW? 51

CHAPTER 5 52
APPLYING PLANT COMMUNICATION 52

- Regenerative Agriculture 52
- Agroforestry: Integrating Trees and Crops 55
- Bioengineered Crops 57
- Sustainable Farming 58
- Did You Know? 60

CHAPTER 6 62

THE PHILOSOPHY OF PLANT LIFE 62

- Recognizing Plant Genius 62
- The Ethics of Plant Life 64
- The Human-Nature Connection 66
- A New Way of Seeing 67
- Did You Know? 69

CHAPTER 7 70

THE FUTURE OF PLANT COMMUNICATION 70

- Emerging Technologies 70
- Climate Change and Plant Resilience 73
- The Role of Education and Awareness 75
- A Call to Action 76
- Did You Know? 78

APPENDICES 80

APPENDIX A 81

- Glossary of Technical Terms 81

APPENDIX B 85

- Timeline of Important Discoveries 85

APPENDIX C 89

- Further Reading and Resources 89

CLASSROOM ACTIVITIES 90

- A Final Word 97

Chapter 1

Mycorrhizal Fungi: The Invisible Network

Introduction

Do you remember standing in the biology lab, adjusting the microscope until that thin leaf slice came into sharp focus? At first, it seemed like a simple fragment of green, but then you noticed the astonishing complexity within. Each cell, vein and tissue layer formed part of an elegant network that carried nutrients, exchanged gases and provided structure. What once appeared to be simple and inert revealed itself as a vibrant microcosm, where every component played a crucial role in sustaining plant life. That was your window into the profound and often mysterious workings hidden inside the plant kingdom.

For centuries, we have regarded plants as passive organisms, that offer comforting and beautiful backdrops to our own dynamic lives. Yet, beneath the verdant canopy and within the roots that anchor our very soil, exists a world brimming with subtle communication, ingenious adaptation, and a level of "intelligence" that is only beginning to be understood by modern science. From the complex dance of photosynthesis to the sophisticated strategies for survival, plants exhibit a scientific intricacy that challenges our conventional understanding of life itself.

This book invites you to embark on a journey into this hidden world, to explore the cutting-edge science that is revealing the remarkable capabilities of plants. Prepare to be amazed by their sensory perceptions, their complex communication networks, their sensitivity and attunement to external stimuli, their ability to learn and remember, and the astonishing secrets they hold within their seemingly simple structures. To use a gardening metaphor, the deeper we dig into the science of plant life, the more we uncover the profound genius that has allowed them to thrive and shape our planet for billions of years. We start, though, at the most obvious place, the world beneath our feet!

The World Beneath Our Feet

The world beneath our feet is far more complex and interconnected than we realize. While the visible parts of plants—leaves, stems, and flowers—are what typically capture our attention, it is the hidden network of mycorrhizal fungi that plays a crucial role in their survival and communication. These fungi form symbiotic relationships with plant roots, creating an underground web that facilitates the exchange of nutrients, water, and even chemical signals. This intricate system, often referred to as the "Wood Wide Web," has been the subject of increasing scientific interest, revealing that plants are not isolated entities but rather part of a vast and dynamic network.

Mycorrhizal fungi constitute a diverse group of organisms that colonize the roots of most terrestrial plants. The word mycorrhizal breaks down into "myco" meaning fungus, "rhiza" meaning root, and the ending "-al" meaning related to—so it basically means "related to a fungus-root relationship." There are two main types of such fungi: ectomycorrhizae and endomycorrhizae. Ectomycorrhizae form a sheath around the root surface, while endomycorrhizae penetrate the root cells themselves. Think of them as external and internal actors. Both these types create a mutualistic relationship with the host plant - the fungi provide the plant with essential minerals and water from the soil, and in return, the plant supplies the fungi with carbohydrates produced through photosynthesis. This exchange is vital for both partners, allowing them to thrive in environments where resources might otherwise be scarce.

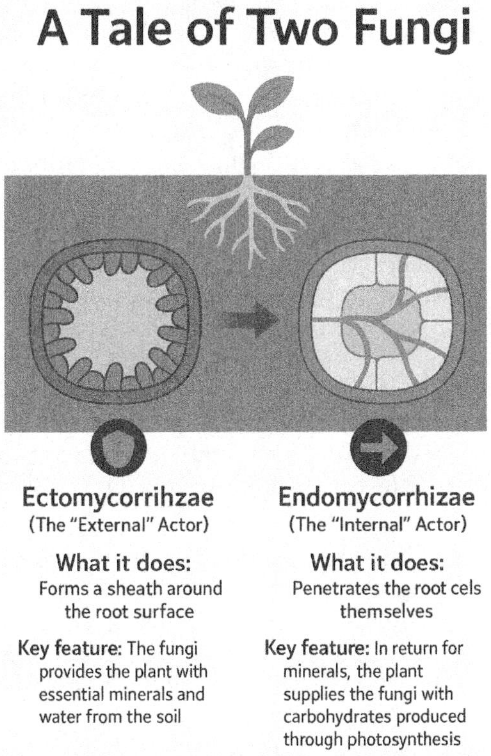

A Tale of Two Fungi

Ectomycorrihzae
(The "External" Actor)

What it does:
Forms a sheath around the root surface

Key feature: The fungi provides the plant with essential minerals and water from the soil

Endomycorrhizae
(The "Internal" Actor)

What it does:
Penetrates the root cels themselves

Key feature: In return for minerals, the plant supplies the fungi with carbohydrates produced through photosynthesis

Fig. 1 Fungi: External versus Internal Actors (Source: Lexicon Labs)

The significance of this network extends beyond mere nutrient exchange. It serves as a conduit for communication between plants, enabling them to share information about environmental conditions, threats, and opportunities. For instance, when a tree is attacked by pests or pathogens, it can release chemical signals that travel through the fungal network, alerting neighboring trees to the danger. This early warning system allows plants to prepare for potential threats, enhancing their chances of survival. Such interactions challenge the traditional view of plants as passive organisms and instead reveal them as active participants in a complex ecosystem.

In addition to facilitating communication, mycorrhizal networks also play a critical role in the resilience of forest ecosystems. Trees within these networks can support one another, especially during times of stress such as drought or nutrient deficiency. Young saplings, which may struggle to establish themselves, can benefit from the resources provided by older, more established trees. This cooperative behavior fosters a sense of community among plants, reinforcing the idea that they are not merely competing for resources but are also working together to ensure the health and vitality of the entire forest.

Moreover, the presence of mycorrhizal fungi can significantly influence the structure and function of the soil. These fungi help to break down organic matter, releasing nutrients that are essential for plant growth. They also contribute to the formation of soil aggregates, improving soil structure and water retention. This process enhances the overall fertility of the soil, making it more conducive to plant life. In agricultural contexts, understanding and harnessing these relationships can lead to more sustainable farming practices, reducing the need for synthetic fertilizers and promoting healthier crops.

As researchers continue to explore the intricacies of mycorrhizal networks, new insights are emerging about the depth of plant communication and cooperation. Studies have shown that these networks can span very large distances, connecting multiple species of plants and even different types of vegetation. For example, in the dense forests of the Pacific Northwest, vast underground fungal networks connect towering Douglas fir trees with neighboring paper birch trees. These different species, one a conifer and the other a broadleaf, engage in a remarkable form of cooperation. The birch trees, which leaf out earlier in the spring, send carbon-based sugars to the young, shaded firs through this shared mycorrhizal web, supplementing their energy when sunlight is scarce. Later in the season, when the firs are photosynthesizing at their peak and the birches may be losing their leaves, the direction of this nutrient flow can reverse. This subterranean exchange demonstrates a complex, large-scale cooperative system where different types of vegetation are intricately linked, ensuring the overall health and resilience of the forest ecosystem. This level of interconnectedness suggests that forests are not just collections of individual trees but are instead complex, interdependent systems where each component plays a vital role in maintaining ecological balance.

The implications of these findings are profound, and are challenging long-held assumptions about the nature of plant life. By recognizing the importance of mycorrhizal fungi, we gain a deeper appreciation for the complexity of the natural world and the ways in which different organisms interact to sustain life. This understanding can inform conservation efforts, guiding us toward more holistic approaches to environmental stewardship. As we continue to uncover the secrets of the underground network, we are reminded that the world beneath our feet is as rich and dynamic as the landscapes we see above.

In short, we can say that the mycorrhizal network represents a fascinating and essential aspect of plant life. Through their symbiotic relationships with fungi, plants engage in a sophisticated exchange of resources and information, forming a web of connections that supports the health of entire ecosystems. This hidden network not only highlights the adaptability and resilience of plants but also underscores the importance of preserving the delicate balance of our natural world. As we delve deeper into the study of these relationships, we are likely to discover even more about the intricate ways in which life on Earth is interconnected.

The Wood Wide Web

This underground network which we just learned about, is composed of mycorrhizal fungi, acts as a vital lifeline for trees and other plants, facilitating the exchange of nutrients, water, and chemical signals. The term "Wood Wide Web" was coined to emphasize the analogy with the internet, highlighting how information and resources flow seamlessly between different organisms, much like data travels across digital networks.

At the heart of this network lies the intricate relationship between fungi and plant roots. The fungi form a symbiotic partnership with the roots, extending their hyphae into the soil to access nutrients and water that would otherwise be out of reach for the plants. In return, the plants supply the fungi with carbohydrates produced through photosynthesis. These relationships are essential for the survival of individual plants and also contribute to the overall health and resilience of the forest ecosystem. The ability of plants to communicate through this network allows them to respond to environmental changes and threats, creating a dynamic and adaptive system.

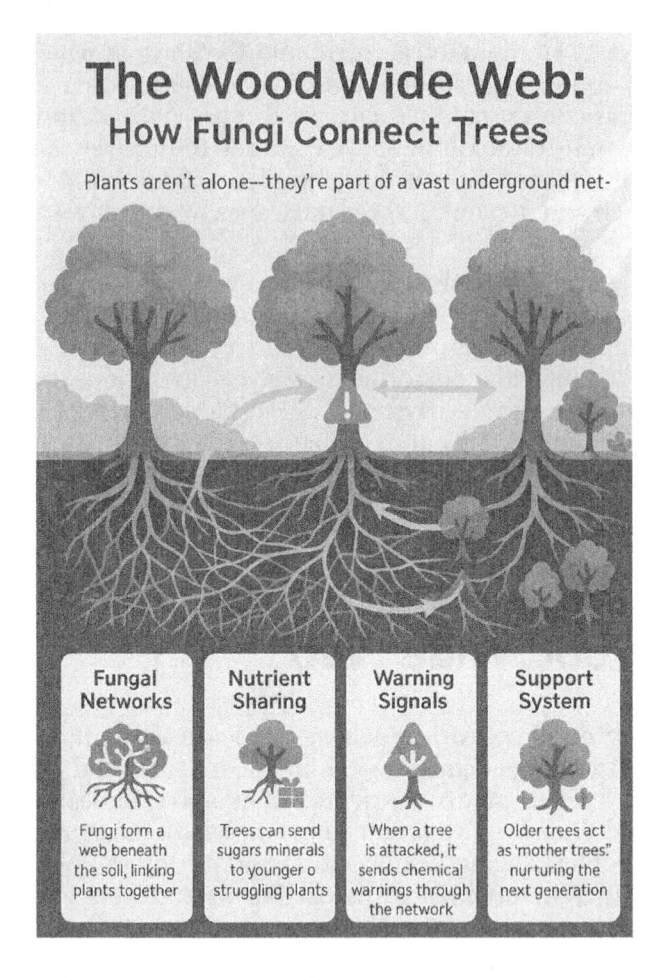

Fig. 2 The Wood Wide Web (Source: Lexicon Labs)

Research has revealed that the Wood Wide Web is not limited to a single species; it connects various types of plants, including trees, shrubs, and even grasses. This interconnectedness enables the sharing of resources and information across different plant species, fostering a sense of community within the forest. For example, when a tree is under attack by pests or disease, it can send chemical signals through the fungal network to alert neighboring plants, prompting them to enhance their defenses. This phenomenon has been observed in several studies, demonstrating the sophistication of plant communication and the critical role that mycorrhizal networks play in maintaining ecological balance.

Moreover, the Wood Wide Web is instrumental in the distribution of nutrients throughout the forest. Older, more established trees, often referred to as "mother trees," can act as hubs within the network, providing resources to younger trees and seedlings. This transfer of nutrients is crucial for the establishment of new growth, particularly in dense forests where competition for light and space can be intense. The ability of mother trees to support their offspring through the fungal network illustrates the complex social dynamics that exist among plants, challenging the notion that they are simply passive organisms.

RESEARCH FOCUS

Plant Communication via Fungal Networks

In a groundbreaking 1997 study published in *Nature*, forest ecologist Suzanne Simard and her team provided the first direct evidence that trees can share resources through underground fungal networks. By tracing carbon isotopes between Douglas fir and paper birch trees, the researchers discovered that carbon moved bidirectionally via shared mycorrhizal fungi—demonstrating that trees do not merely compete for resources but actively cooperate across species. This finding overturned long-held assumptions about forest dynamics and introduced the concept of the "Wood Wide Web," revealing that forests function more like interconnected communities than isolated individuals. The study reshaped ecological thinking and influenced sustainable forestry practices worldwide.

The importance of the Wood Wide Web extends beyond the immediate benefits of nutrient exchange and communication. It also plays a vital role in the resilience of forest ecosystems in the face of environmental stressors. As climate change alters weather patterns and increases the frequency of extreme events, the interconnectedness of plants through mycorrhizal networks can enhance their ability to withstand these challenges. By sharing resources and information, plants can collectively adapt to changing conditions, ensuring the survival of the entire ecosystem.

Understanding how plants interact through these networks can inform strategies for reforestation and habitat restoration. By promoting the growth of diverse plant species and encouraging the development of healthy mycorrhizal networks, land managers can enhance the resilience of ecosystems and promote biodiversity. This approach not only supports the health of individual plants but also contributes to the overall stability of the environment.

In addition to its ecological significance, the Wood Wide Web has sparked interest in the broader implications for human society. As we become increasingly aware of the interconnectedness of all living things, there is a growing recognition of the importance of protecting and preserving these networks. The lessons learned from the Wood Wide Web can inspire a shift in our relationship with nature, encouraging us to adopt more sustainable practices and foster a deeper appreciation for the intricate systems that support life on Earth.

The Wood Wide Web thus represents a remarkable example of the interconnectedness of plant life, facilitated by the intricate relationships between mycorrhizal fungi and plant roots. This global underground network not only supports the survival and growth of individual plants but also enhances the resilience of entire ecosystems. As we continue to explore the complexities of these relationships, we gain valuable insights into the ways in which life on Earth is intertwined, reminding us of the importance of nurturing and protecting the delicate balance of our natural world.

Communication Through the Fungal Network

One of the most well-documented examples of plant communication through the fungal network is the exchange of chemical warnings. When a tree is attacked by herbivores or infected by pathogens, it releases specific volatile compounds into the air, which can be detected by nearby plants. However, the fungal network provides an additional layer of communication by transmitting these chemical signals directly through the roots. This allows plants to receive warnings more efficiently and react before they are exposed to the same threat. For instance, when a Douglas fir is damaged by insects, it releases a compound that travels through the fungal network, triggering defensive responses in neighboring trees. This early warning system helps plants prepare for potential attacks, increasing their chances of survival.

In addition to warning signals, the fungal network also plays a crucial role in the transfer of nutrients and other biochemical compounds. Plants can use this network to share resources, particularly in situations where certain species may be struggling to obtain sufficient nutrients. This exchange is not random but rather a strategic process that ensures the overall health of the ecosystem. For example, older trees can channel excess sugars and minerals to younger or weaker plants, helping them grow and develop more effectively. This kind of resource sharing is especially important in dense forests where competition for sunlight and nutrients is fierce. By supporting each other through the fungal network, plants can maintain a balanced and thriving environment.

Another fascinating aspect of plant communication through the fungal network is the ability of plants to recognize and respond to the presence of other species. Research has shown that some plants can distinguish between the roots of different species and adjust their interactions accordingly. This selective communication allows plants to form beneficial relationships while avoiding potentially harmful ones. For instance, certain plants may release chemicals that inhibit the growth of invasive species, while others may encourage the growth of beneficial fungi that enhance nutrient uptake. This level of interaction demonstrates that plants are not only capable of responding to their environment but also of shaping it through their communication strategies.

The mechanisms behind this communication are still being studied, but scientists have identified several key components that facilitate the exchange of information. One of the primary methods involves the release of signaling molecules such as flavonoids, terpenoids, and phenolic compounds. These substances can travel through the fungal hyphae and trigger physiological responses in recipient plants. Additionally, the presence of specific enzymes and proteins within the fungal network may help regulate the flow of information, ensuring that signals are transmitted accurately and efficiently.

Understanding how plants communicate through the fungal network has significant implications for both ecological research and practical applications. By studying these interactions, scientists can gain insights into the complex relationships that govern plant communities and develop more effective strategies for conservation and sustainable agriculture. Furthermore, this knowledge can inspire new approaches to managing ecosystems, emphasizing the importance of maintaining healthy mycorrhizal networks to support plant health and resilience.

As research continues to uncover the intricacies of plant communication, it becomes increasingly clear that the fungal network is far more than a simple transportation system for nutrients. It is a dynamic and intelligent network that enables plants to share information, collaborate, and adapt to their surroundings. This discovery challenges traditional views of plant life and highlights the remarkable complexity of the natural world. By recognizing the role of the fungal network in plant communication, we gain a deeper appreciation for the interconnectedness of all living things and the importance of preserving these vital relationships.

Why This Matters?

The discovery of plant communication through the fungal network has profound implications for both ecology and agriculture, reshaping our understanding of how ecosystems function and how we can cultivate food more sustainably. As we discussed at the outset, traditionally, plants have been viewed as independent organisms that compete for resources, but the evidence of their interconnectedness through mycorrhizal networks reveals a more cooperative and dynamic system. This realization has significant consequences for how we manage natural environments and how we approach agricultural practices.

In ecological terms, the fungal network plays a critical role in maintaining the stability and resilience of forest ecosystems. The ability of plants to share resources, warn each other of threats, and support one another in times of stress contributes to the overall health of the environment. This interconnectedness helps forests withstand disturbances such as droughts, pest outbreaks, and climate fluctuations. By understanding and preserving these networks, conservationists can develop more effective strategies for protecting biodiversity and restoring degraded landscapes. For example, reforestation efforts that incorporate diverse plant species and promote the growth of mycorrhizal fungi can enhance the resilience of newly planted forests, ensuring their long-term survival.

Beyond conservation, the insights gained from studying plant communication have direct applications in agriculture. Traditional farming methods often rely heavily on synthetic fertilizers and pesticides to boost crop yields and protect against pests. However, these practices can disrupt the natural balance of soil ecosystems and reduce the effectiveness of mycorrhizal networks. By adopting more sustainable approaches that work with the existing fungal networks, farmers can improve soil health, increase nutrient availability, and reduce the need for chemical inputs. Techniques such as cover cropping, reduced tillage, and the use of organic amendments can help maintain and enhance these underground connections, leading to more resilient and productive agricultural systems.

Additionally, the concept of agroforestry—integrating trees and shrubs into agricultural landscapes—has gained traction as a way to mimic the natural interactions found in forests. By planting crops alongside trees, farmers can create a more balanced environment where plants can share resources and support each other through the fungal network. This approach not only improves soil fertility and water retention but also enhances biodiversity and reduces the risk of crop failure. As the demand for sustainable food production grows, these practices offer promising alternatives to conventional farming methods that prioritize short-term yield over long-term ecological health.

The implications of plant communication extend beyond individual farms and forests, influencing broader discussions about environmental policy and land management. Governments and organizations are beginning to recognize the importance of preserving and restoring mycorrhizal networks as part of larger conservation efforts. Policies that promote sustainable land use, protect native plant species, and encourage the use of regenerative agricultural techniques can help maintain the integrity of these networks. By integrating scientific knowledge with practical applications, we can develop more holistic approaches to environmental stewardship that benefit both ecosystems and human societies.

Ultimately, the study of plant communication through the fungal network highlights the intricate and often overlooked relationships that sustain life on Earth. As we continue to explore these connections, we gain valuable insights into how to better manage and protect our natural resources. Whether in the wild or in cultivated fields, the ability of plants to communicate and cooperate through the Wood Wide Web offers a powerful reminder of the complexity and resilience of the natural world. By embracing this knowledge, we can move toward a future where agriculture and ecology work in harmony, ensuring the health and sustainability of our planet for generations to come.

Did You Know?

Trees can send sugars to unrelated species—birch trees have been shown to feed Douglas fir saplings through fungal networks when sunlight is scarce.

Plants issue underground warnings—when insect attack, some trees send chemical signals through the fungi to alert their neighbors.

Fungi basically act like internet routers—the "Wood Wide Web" connects trees across vast distances, including different species like grasses, shrubs, and conifers.

Fungal networks shape soil structure—they improve water retention and soil aggregation, boosting fertility without synthetic fertilizers.

Plants can detect and reject intruders—some can recognize non-native roots and selectively block communication through their fungal channels.

Chapter 2

The Language of Smells

Plant Communication

Plant communication is the way in which plants share information with each other and with other organisms. It is not like human speech or animal calls. Instead, plants use chemicals, electrical signals, and underground networks of fungi. These methods help plants warn their neighbors of danger, share resources when times are tough, and even influence the behavior of insects and other animals.

When a leaf is chewed by an insect or infected by a pathogen, the damaged plant releases a mix of odor molecules into the air. These molecules are called volatile organic compounds. Neighboring plants detect the blend and begin to activate their own defenses. They may strengthen their cell walls, produce bitter chemicals, or release signals that attract predators of the herbivore. This response can happen within minutes of the first damage, giving nearby plants a head start on protecting themselves. Plants also rely on electrical signals to send rapid alerts within their own bodies. If one part of a plant is hurt, a change in electrical charge travels through the vascular system like a wave. That wave triggers the production of defense hormones in distant leaves and stems. The result is a coordinated reaction across the whole plant, not just at the injury site. These electrical signals move more slowly than those in animal nerves, but they are fast enough to mount an effective defense.

PLANT COMMUNICATION IN ACTION
HOW PLANTS TALK TO EACH OTHER

Plants have their own language—here's how they share information.

CHEMICAL SIGNALS
(Volatile Compounds)

When a plant is attacked, it releases chemicals to warn others.

Tomoto plants releasing chemicals when aphids attack

FUNGAL NETWORKS
(The Wood Wide Web)

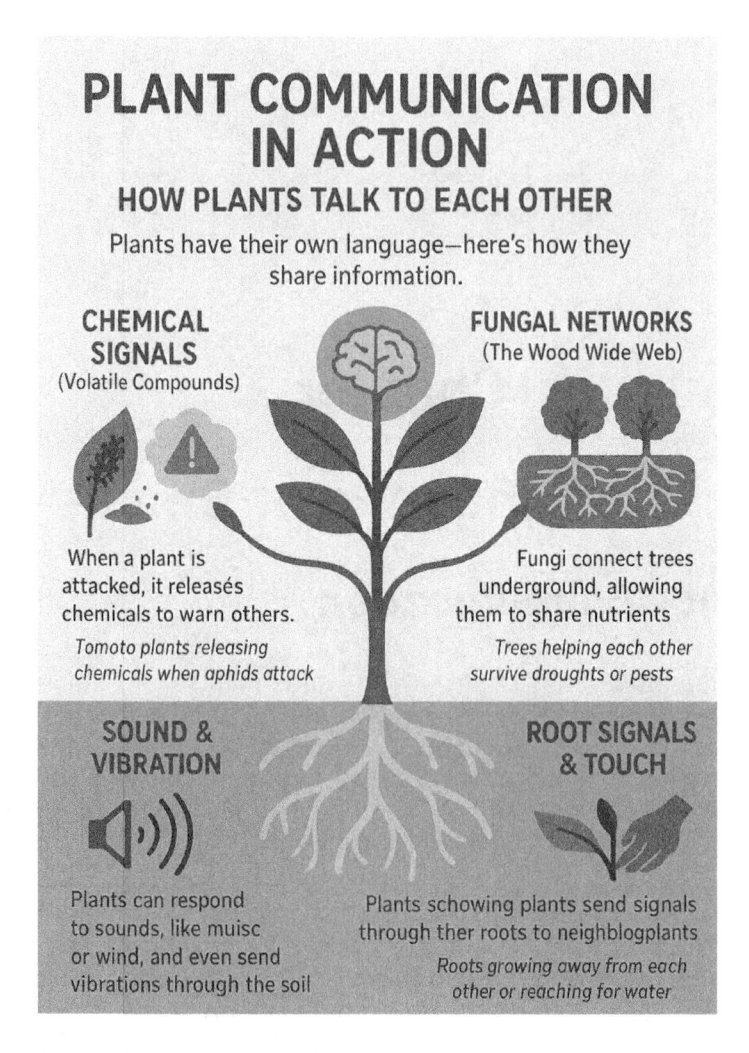

Fungi connect trees underground, allowing them to share nutrients

Trees helping each other survive droughts or pests

SOUND & VIBRATION

Plants can respond to sounds, like muisc or wind, and even send vibrations through the soil

ROOT SIGNALS & TOUCH

Plants schowing plants send signals through ther roots to neighbloglplants

Roots growing away from each other or reaching for water

Fig. 3 Plant Communication (Source: Lexicon Labs)

Below the surface, a vast network of fungal threads links the roots of many plants. These mycorrhizal fungi form relationships with roots in exchange for sugars. In turn, the fungi extend far through the soil, creating a shared web. Through this web, a plant under stress—such as drought or disease—can send warning cues to other plants. Neighboring plants then adjust their water use or grow stronger root systems in response. Some large "hub" trees even act as information centers, storing extra nutrients and passing them on to younger plants.

Understanding plant communication has many practical benefits. Farmers might breed crops that emit clearer or stronger warning signals. This could reduce the need for chemical pesticides by drawing natural enemies of pests. Planting mixtures of related varieties could improve resistance to drought or disease, since they share information more effectively through fungal networks. Scientists are also exploring ways to trigger electrical signaling with harmless stimuli so crops can prepare for threats without spraying chemicals.

Ongoing research uses advanced imaging tools, genetic analysis, and computer models to map out these communication channels in greater detail. As knowledge grows, it may change how agriculture, forestry, and conservation work. Seeing plants as active participants in their environment highlights their remarkable ability to sense, respond, and even cooperate—qualities that expand our understanding of intelligence in the natural world.

In this chapter, we will consider the language of smells in more detail.

The Role of VOCs

As we already know, plants are highly responsive to their environment. One of the most fascinating ways they interact with the world around them is through chemical signals that serve as a form of communication. These chemical messages allow plants to warn neighbors of danger, attract pollinators, and even regulate their own growth and development. This intricate system of chemical signaling plays a crucial role in plant survival and has significant implications for both ecological interactions and agricultural practices.

At the heart of this communication is the release of volatile organic compounds (VOCs), which are chemical substances that evaporate easily and can travel through the air. When a plant is under stress—whether from herbivore attacks, disease, or environmental changes—it releases specific VOCs that act as alarm signals. These signals can be detected by neighboring plants, triggering defensive responses such as the production of toxic compounds or the reinforcement of cell walls. This ability to communicate through scent allows plants to prepare for potential threats before they are directly affected, enhancing their chances of survival.

One of the most well-documented examples of this phenomenon is the response of tomato plants to insect infestations. When a tomato plant is attacked by aphids, it releases a blend of VOCs that signal nearby plants to increase their production of defensive chemicals. This early warning system not only helps the affected plant defend itself more effectively but also alerts surrounding plants to take similar precautions. Such interactions demonstrate how chemical signaling is not just a means of self-preservation but also a way for plants to support one another within a shared ecosystem.

RESEARCH FOCUS

Plants Emitting Airborne Chemical Warnings

A seminal 1983 experiment by David Rhoades at the University of Washington revealed that willow trees attacked by tent caterpillars began producing defensive chemicals not only in the affected leaves but also in nearby, untouched trees. The study demonstrated that plants release airborne chemical signals—now known as volatile organic compounds (VOCs)—that can trigger defense mechanisms in neighboring plants. This discovery provided the first concrete evidence of above-ground plant communication and helped shift the scientific view of plants from passive organisms to responsive, signaling entities. It laid the foundation for the field of chemical ecology and remains a cornerstone in our understanding of plant intelligence.

In addition to defending against pests, chemical signals also play a vital role in attracting pollinators. Many flowering plants rely on scent to lure bees, butterflies, and other insects to their blossoms. These scents are often composed of complex mixtures of volatile compounds that vary between species, allowing pollinators to recognize and locate the flowers they depend on for food. For example, the sweet fragrance of jasmine or the strong aroma of lavender can attract specific pollinators, ensuring the successful transfer of pollen and the continuation of plant reproduction.

The use of chemical signals is not limited to above-ground interactions; it also extends beneath the soil, where root exudates play a critical role in plant communication. Root exudates are organic compounds released by plant roots into the surrounding soil, and they serve multiple functions. Some of these exudates act as signals to beneficial microbes, encouraging the growth of symbiotic fungi and bacteria that help the plant absorb nutrients more efficiently. Others function as chemical messengers, alerting neighboring plants to changes in soil conditions or the presence of pathogens.

This underground communication system is particularly important in maintaining the health of plant communities. In forests, for instance, trees can use root exudates to share information about nutrient availability, helping younger or weaker plants access essential resources. This kind of interplant signaling contributes to the overall resilience of the ecosystem, reinforcing the idea that plants are not isolated entities but rather part of a larger, interconnected network.

Another significant aspect of chemical signaling in plants is its role in defense against herbivores. Some plants produce strong-smelling compounds that deter animals from feeding on them. For example, the pungent scent of garlic or the sharp aroma of mint can repel insects and other herbivores, reducing the likelihood of damage. These natural defenses are an evolutionary adaptation that allows plants to survive in environments where predation is a constant threat.

In addition to deterring herbivores, some plants use chemical signals to manipulate the behavior of their predators. Certain species release volatile compounds that attract the natural enemies of herbivores, creating a form of indirect defense. For instance, when a plant is attacked by caterpillars, it may release chemicals that attract parasitic wasps, which then lay their eggs inside the caterpillars, ultimately killing them. This sophisticated strategy highlights the complexity of plant communication and the ways in which plants have evolved to protect themselves through chemical interactions.

The study of plant chemical signaling has also led to new insights in agriculture and pest management. By understanding how plants use VOCs to communicate, scientists and farmers can develop more effective strategies for protecting crops without relying heavily on synthetic pesticides. For example, researchers have explored the use of plant-based repellents that mimic the natural scents of certain plants, reducing the need for chemical interventions. Additionally, the ability to detect and interpret plant signals could lead to the development of early warning systems that alert farmers to potential threats, such as pest infestations or disease outbreaks.

Despite the growing body of research on plant chemical signaling, many aspects of this process remain poorly understood. Scientists continue to investigate the specific compounds involved, the mechanisms of detection, and the ways in which different plant species respond to chemical cues. Advances in analytical techniques, such as gas chromatography and mass spectrometry, have made it possible to identify and quantify the volatile compounds produced by plants, providing valuable data for further study.

As our understanding of plant communication deepens, it becomes increasingly clear that chemical signaling is a fundamental aspect of plant life. From the exchange of nutrients through root exudates to the use of VOCs for defense and attraction, these chemical messages shape the interactions between plants and their environment. By studying these processes, we gain a greater appreciation for the complexity of the natural world and the ways in which plants have adapted to thrive in diverse ecosystems.

Ultimately, the language of smells is a powerful reminder of the intelligence and adaptability of plant life. It challenges the notion that plants are passive organisms and instead reveals them as active participants in a dynamic and interconnected system. As we continue to explore the intricacies of chemical signaling, we open the door to new possibilities for sustainable agriculture, ecological conservation, and a deeper understanding of the natural world.

Volatile Compounds and Plant Defense

The use of volatile compounds by plants is a remarkable example of how they employ chemical signaling for defense against herbivores and pathogens. These compounds, known as volatile organic compounds (VOCs), are released into the air and serve as a form of communication that alerts neighboring plants to potential threats. This mechanism is particularly effective because it allows plants to react to dangers before they are directly impacted, thereby increasing their chances of survival.

When a plant is under attack, such as by herbivorous insects or pathogenic microorganisms, it begins to release specific VOCs that act as distress signals. These signals can be detected by other plants in the vicinity, prompting them to initiate defensive measures. For instance, when a tomato plant is attacked by aphids, it emits a blend of VOCs that can be sensed by neighboring plants. This early warning system enables those plants to enhance their own defenses, such as producing toxic compounds or reinforcing their cellular structures, thus making them less vulnerable to the same type of attack. This collective response not only benefits the individual plant being attacked but also strengthens the entire community of plants, illustrating the importance of chemical signaling in fostering resilience within ecosystems.

Moreover, the release of VOCs is not solely a reaction to direct threats; it also plays a role in attracting natural predators of herbivores. This dual function of chemical signaling highlights the complexity of plant interactions. For example, when a plant is damaged by caterpillars, it may emit VOCs that attract parasitic wasps. These wasps lay their eggs inside the caterpillars, which eventually leads to the death of the herbivores. This form of indirect defense showcases how plants can manipulate their environment to their advantage, using chemical signals to create a web of relationships that benefit the entire ecosystem.

In addition to defending against herbivores, plants also utilize chemical signals to combat diseases. When a plant is infected by a pathogen, it can release specific VOCs that signal the presence of the infection to neighboring plants. This early warning allows those plants to activate their immune responses, such as producing antimicrobial compounds or altering their metabolic processes to resist the pathogen. This proactive approach to disease management is crucial for maintaining the health of plant populations, especially in dense forests where the spread of disease can be rapid and devastating.

The effectiveness of volatile compounds in plant defense is further enhanced by the diversity of these compounds. Different plant species produce unique blends of VOCs, which can serve various purposes depending on the context. For example, some plants release strong-smelling compounds that act as deterrents to herbivores, while others produce subtle scents that attract pollinators. This variability allows plants to tailor their chemical signals to their specific needs, maximizing their chances of survival and reproductive success.

Research into the role of VOCs in plant defense has also revealed the potential for applications in agriculture. By understanding how plants use these chemical signals, scientists can develop strategies to enhance crop resilience and reduce the reliance on synthetic pesticides. For instance, farmers can cultivate plant varieties that naturally emit higher levels of defensive VOCs, thereby reducing the need for chemical interventions. Additionally, the use of bioengineered plants that can produce specific VOCs to attract beneficial insects or repel pests offers promising avenues for sustainable farming practices.

The study of plant chemical signaling has implications beyond individual plant defense. It provides insights into the broader ecological dynamics that govern plant communities. The ability of plants to communicate through VOCs influences the interactions between different species, shaping the structure and function of ecosystems. For example, the release of VOCs can affect the behavior of herbivores, influencing their feeding patterns and distribution across a landscape. This, in turn, can impact the health and diversity of plant populations, highlighting the interconnectedness of all living organisms.

As our understanding of plant chemical signaling continues to evolve, it becomes increasingly evident that the use of volatile compounds is a vital component of plant survival. These chemical signals enable plants to respond to threats, attract allies, and maintain the balance of their ecosystems. By recognizing the significance of these interactions, we can better appreciate the complexity of plant life and the intricate relationships that exist within the natural world. This knowledge not only enhances our scientific understanding but also informs practical applications that promote sustainable agriculture and ecological conservation. Through continued research and application, we can harness the power of chemical signaling to foster healthier, more resilient plant communities.

The Language of Smells: How Plants Use Chemical Signals

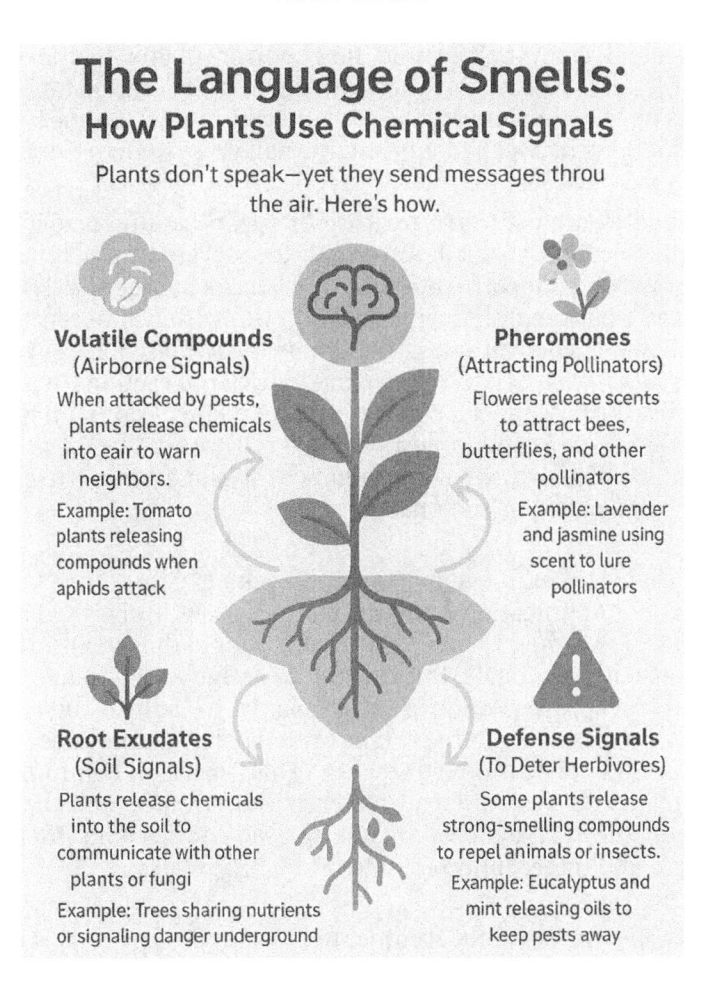

Plants don't speak—yet they send messages throu the air. Here's how.

Volatile Compounds
(Airborne Signals)
When attacked by pests, plants release chemicals into eair to warn neighbors.
Example: Tomato plants releasing compounds when aphids attack

Pheromones
(Attracting Pollinators)
Flowers release scents to attract bees, butterflies, and other pollinators
Example: Lavender and jasmine using scent to lure pollinators

Root Exudates
(Soil Signals)
Plants release chemicals into the soil to communicate with other plants or fungi
Example: Trees sharing nutrients or signaling danger underground

Defense Signals
(To Deter Herbivores)
Some plants release strong-smelling compounds to repel animals or insects.
Example: Eucalyptus and mint releasing oils to keep pests away

Fig. 4 The Language of Smells (Source: Lexicon Labs)

Root Exudates: Signals Beneath the Soil

While volatile compounds play a crucial role in above-ground plant communication, the underground world is equally rich in chemical signaling. One of the most significant forms of below-ground communication occurs through root exudates—organic compounds released by plant roots into the surrounding soil. These exudates serve as chemical messages that influence not only the plant itself but also the microbial communities and neighboring plants in the vicinity. Unlike the airborne signals that can travel over long distances, root exudates operate in a more localized and continuous manner, shaping the interactions between plants and the soil ecosystem.

Root exudates are a diverse mixture of sugars, amino acids, organic acids, and secondary metabolites that are secreted by plant roots as they grow and absorb nutrients. These compounds can vary significantly between plant species and even within different parts of the same plant. Their primary function is to facilitate nutrient uptake, but they also play a key role in mediating interactions with other organisms. For instance, certain root exudates can stimulate the growth of beneficial microbes, such as nitrogen-fixing bacteria and mycorrhizal fungi, which in turn enhance the plant's access to essential nutrients like nitrogen and phosphorus.

Beyond their role in nutrient acquisition, root exudates also serve as a means of communication between plants. When a plant experiences stress—such as drought, nutrient deficiency, or pathogen attack—it can release specific exudates that signal to neighboring plants. These chemical cues can prompt nearby plants to adjust their growth patterns, increase their production of defensive compounds, or alter their resource allocation strategies. This form of communication allows plants to respond collectively to environmental challenges, reinforcing the idea that they are not isolated entities but rather part of a dynamic and interconnected network.

One of the most well-documented examples of root exudate communication involves the interaction between leguminous plants and nitrogen-fixing bacteria. Legumes release flavonoids and other signaling molecules that attract rhizobia, a group of bacteria that colonize their roots and convert atmospheric nitrogen into a form that the plant can use. This mutualistic relationship is essential for maintaining soil fertility, as it reduces the need for synthetic fertilizers and supports the growth of other plant species. However, the communication between plants and microbes is not limited to legumes; many other plant species engage in similar interactions with beneficial fungi and bacteria that help them acquire nutrients and resist diseases.

In addition to facilitating symbiotic relationships, root exudates also play a role in plant competition. Some plants release allelopathic compounds—chemicals that inhibit the growth of neighboring plants—

through their roots. This strategy allows them to dominate specific areas of the soil and limit the availability of resources for other species. A classic example of this is the black walnut tree (Juglans nigra), which secretes juglone, a compound that suppresses the growth of many other plants. This form of chemical warfare ensures that the black walnut maintains a competitive advantage in its ecosystem.

The ability of plants to communicate through root exudates has significant implications for both ecological and agricultural practices. In natural ecosystems, these chemical signals contribute to the maintenance of biodiversity by regulating plant interactions and promoting the coexistence of different species. In agricultural settings, understanding and harnessing these interactions can lead to more sustainable farming methods. By cultivating plant species that produce beneficial root exudates, farmers can improve soil health, enhance nutrient cycling, and reduce the need for chemical inputs. Techniques such as cover cropping and intercropping can also be used to optimize the exchange of root exudates and promote a more balanced and resilient agroecosystem.

Despite the growing body of research on root exudates, many aspects of this complex system remain poorly understood. Scientists are still investigating the specific compounds involved, the mechanisms of detection, and the ways in which different plant species respond to chemical cues. Advances in analytical techniques, such as high-performance liquid chromatography and molecular profiling, have made it possible to identify and quantify the diverse range of compounds present in root exudates, providing valuable insights into their functions and interactions.

As our understanding of plant communication continues to expand, it becomes increasingly clear that root exudates are a vital component of the underground network that connects plant life. These chemical signals not only influence the growth and survival of individual plants but also shape the broader dynamics of the soil ecosystem. By studying these interactions, we gain a deeper appreciation for the complexity of the natural world and the intricate relationships that sustain life on Earth.

Attracting Allies: Pheromones and Pollination

In addition to their roles in defense and resource sharing, plants also use chemical signals to attract pollinators, ensuring the continuation of their reproductive cycles. This process is largely facilitated by pheromones—specific chemical compounds that act as signals to guide pollinators such as bees, butterflies, and birds toward flowers. Unlike the volatile compounds used for defense, which are primarily released in response to threats, pheromones are designed to attract and communicate with specific organisms that aid in plant reproduction. This intricate system of chemical communication plays a crucial role in maintaining the balance of ecosystems and supporting the survival of both plants and their pollinators.

Flowers have evolved a wide variety of scents to attract different types of pollinators, each tailored to the preferences of its target species. For example, the sweet and intoxicating fragrance of jasmine is highly attractive to moths, while the strong, spicy scent of orchids appeals to certain species of bees. These scents are composed of complex mixtures of volatile organic compounds that can be detected by the olfactory systems of pollinators. By releasing these specific chemical signals, plants ensure that they are visited by the most effective pollinators, increasing the chances of successful fertilization and seed production.

One of the most well-known examples of chemical communication in pollination is the relationship between honeybees and flowering plants. Bees are drawn to flowers by their colors, shapes, and scents, with the latter playing a particularly important role in guiding them to nectar-rich blooms. Research has shown that flowers can modify their scent profiles based on the time of day, the availability of nectar, and the presence of other pollinators, demonstrating a level of adaptability that enhances their chances of being pollinated. This dynamic interaction between plants and pollinators highlights the sophistication of chemical signaling in the natural world.

In addition to attracting pollinators, some plants use pheromones to communicate with other organisms that contribute to their reproductive success. For instance, certain species of orchids produce chemical compounds that mimic the pheromones of female insects, tricking male pollinators into attempting to mate with the flower. This deceptive strategy, known as pseudocopulation, ensures that the orchid is pollinated without offering any reward to the insect. While this method may seem unusual, it is an effective way for plants to secure pollination in environments where traditional pollinators may be scarce.

The role of pheromones in pollination is not limited to insects; some plants also rely on birds and bats for pollination. These animals are attracted to flowers with strong, musky scents or those that bloom at night, such as the large, white flowers of the night-blooming cereus. The scent of these flowers is often described as sweet or fruity, appealing to the olfactory senses of nocturnal pollinators. By adapting their chemical signals to suit the preferences of different pollinators, plants maximize their chances of successful reproduction and ensure the continuation of their genetic lineage.

The study of plant pheromones and their role in pollination has important implications for both ecological research and agricultural practices. Understanding the chemical cues that attract pollinators can help scientists develop strategies to enhance pollination efficiency, particularly in regions where pollinator populations are declining due to habitat loss, pesticide use, and climate change. By cultivating plant species that produce specific pheromones, farmers and gardeners can encourage the presence of beneficial pollinators, leading to improved crop yields and more sustainable agricultural systems.

Moreover, the knowledge gained from studying plant-pollinator interactions can inform conservation efforts aimed at protecting endangered pollinator species. Many pollinators, such as bees and butterflies, are experiencing population declines due to various environmental pressures. By identifying the chemical signals that attract these species, conservationists can design habitats that provide suitable food sources and nesting sites, helping to restore their populations and maintain the delicate balance of ecosystems.

As research into plant communication continues to advance, the role of pheromones in pollination remains a fascinating area of study. These chemical signals not only facilitate the reproductive success of plants but also highlight the intricate relationships that exist between different species. By recognizing the importance of these interactions, we gain a deeper appreciation for the complexity of the natural world and the ways in which life on Earth is interconnected. This understanding can inspire more thoughtful approaches to conservation, agriculture, and environmental stewardship, ensuring the long-term health and sustainability of our planet's ecosystems.

Keeping Pests at Bay

In addition to their role in attracting pollinators, plants also use chemical signals to deter herbivores and protect themselves from potential threats. One of the most effective ways they achieve this is through the release of strong-smelling compounds that act as natural repellents. These defensive scents serve as a first line of defense, discouraging animals and insects from feeding on the plant and reducing the risk of damage. This form of chemical signaling is a crucial adaptation that allows plants to survive in environments where predation is a constant challenge.

Many plants have evolved to produce volatile compounds that are either unpleasant to herbivores or toxic to them. For example, the strong, pungent scent of garlic and onions is not only familiar to humans but also serves as a deterrent to insects and mammals that might otherwise feed on these plants. Similarly, the sharp, menthol-like aroma of mint is known to repel a wide range of pests, including ants, mosquitoes, and even larger animals like deer. These natural defenses are not only effective but also environmentally friendly, offering an alternative to synthetic pesticides that can harm non-target species and disrupt ecosystems.

The use of defensive scents is not limited to individual plants; some species have developed strategies that involve manipulating the behavior of their predators. For instance, when a plant is attacked by herbivores, it may release specific volatile compounds that attract the natural enemies of those herbivores. This indirect form of defense is particularly effective in reducing the impact of pests on plant populations. For example, when a tomato plant is damaged by caterpillars, it can release chemicals that attract parasitic wasps, which then lay their eggs inside the caterpillars, ultimately killing them. This intricate interaction demonstrates how plants can use chemical signals to create a web of relationships that benefit the entire ecosystem.

In addition to deterring herbivores, some plants use their defensive scents to ward off pathogens and disease-causing organisms. Certain species produce antimicrobial compounds that not only protect them from infection but also help prevent the spread of disease to neighboring plants. For instance, the strong, woody scent of eucalyptus is known to have antifungal and antibacterial properties, making it an effective defense against a variety of plant pathogens. By releasing these compounds, plants can maintain their health and reduce the risk of widespread infection, which is particularly important in densely populated plant communities.

The effectiveness of defensive scents has also been observed in agricultural settings, where farmers and researchers are exploring ways to harness these natural defenses to improve crop resilience. By selecting plant varieties that naturally produce higher levels of defensive compounds, growers can reduce the need for chemical pesticides and promote more sustainable farming practices. Additionally, the development of bioengineered plants that can release specific defensive scents in response to herbivore activity offers promising solutions for managing pest populations without harming the environment.

Understanding the role of defensive scents in plant survival has significant implications for both ecological and agricultural research. By studying how plants use chemical signals to protect themselves, scientists can gain insights into the complex interactions that shape plant communities and inform the development of more effective pest management strategies. Furthermore, this knowledge can inspire new approaches to sustainable agriculture, emphasizing the importance of working with nature rather than against it to ensure the long-term health of our ecosystems.

As research into plant chemical signaling continues to advance, the study of defensive scents remains a vital area of exploration. These natural defenses not only highlight the adaptability and resilience of plant life but also underscore the intricate relationships that exist between plants, animals, and the environment. By recognizing the importance of these chemical signals, we can develop more informed strategies for protecting plant health, preserving biodiversity, and fostering a more sustainable future for our planet.

Did You Know?

Plants can "eavesdrop" on their neighbors—some detect stress signals from nearby damaged plants and preemptively activate defenses before being attacked.

Some flowers mimic insect pheromones—certain orchids trick male bees into pollinating them by imitating the scent of female bees.

Plants use underground 'chemical whispers'—root exudates not only recruit beneficial fungi but also warn neighboring roots of soil pathogens.

Tomato plants call in bodyguards—when attacked by caterpillars, they release VOCs that attract parasitic wasps to eliminate the threat.

Floral scents change throughout the day—many flowers adjust their fragrance depending on the time to align with pollinator behavior, thus optimizing visits.

Chapter 3
The Science of Plant Sensitivity

Plants are Super-Sensors

Plants have long been perceived as passive organisms, but scientific research has revealed that they are far more sensitive to their environment than previously thought. Unlike animals, which rely on complex nervous systems and sensory organs to detect external stimuli, plants use a combination of chemical, mechanical, and electromagnetic responses to perceive and react to their surroundings. This ability to sense and respond to changes in light, temperature, moisture, and even sound challenges the traditional view of plants as static entities and highlights the sophisticated ways in which they interact with the world around them.

One of the most fundamental aspects of plant sensitivity is their ability to detect and respond to light. Plants use specialized photoreceptor proteins to sense different wavelengths of light, allowing them to regulate processes such as photosynthesis, growth, and flowering. For example, phytochromes are responsible for detecting red and far-red light, influencing seed germination and leaf expansion. Cryptochromes, on the other hand, respond to blue and ultraviolet light, playing a role in circadian rhythms and phototropism—the directional growth of plants toward or away from a light source. These light-sensitive mechanisms enable plants to optimize their energy capture and adapt to changing environmental conditions.

How Do Plants 'Listen'?
The Surprising Ways They Hear and Feel

Plants may not have ears—but they can still sense the world around them.

Sound & Music
Some studies show plants respond to certain frequencies or even recognize their owner's voice

Vibrations in the Soil
Plants can detect vibrations throuch their roots—like when animals walk nearby or water flows

Wind and Air Movement
Plants use wind as a signal—like when they grow toward light or bend to avoid damage

Touch and Physical Contact
Plants can sense when something touches them and react accordingly

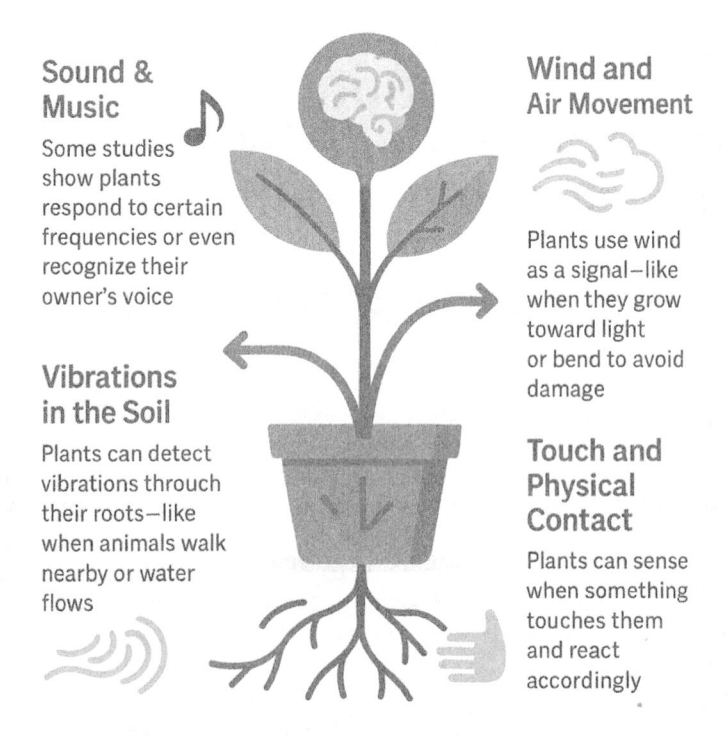

Fig. 5 How Plants Listen (Source: Lexicon Labs)

In addition to light, plants are also highly responsive to temperature fluctuations. Many species can detect subtle changes in temperature through specialized proteins that trigger physiological responses. For instance, some plants use cold sensing to determine when to flower or go dormant, while others adjust their metabolic rates in response to heat stress. This temperature sensitivity allows plants to survive in diverse climates and ensures their continued growth and reproduction under varying environmental conditions.

Another crucial aspect of plant sensitivity is their ability to detect and respond to touch. While it may seem counterintuitive, plants can sense physical contact and react accordingly. This phenomenon, known as thigmotropism, is evident in climbing plants that wrap around supports or vines that curl when touched. The mechanism behind this response involves the activation of mechanosensitive ion channels in plant cells, which trigger changes in cell elongation and direction of growth. Some plants, such as the Venus flytrap, even exhibit rapid movements in response to touch, closing their traps within seconds to capture prey.

Beyond these well-documented forms of sensitivity, emerging research suggests that plants may also be capable of detecting and responding to sound. Although they lack ears or auditory organs, studies have shown that plants can perceive vibrations and acoustic signals, leading to measurable physiological changes. For example, experiments have demonstrated that certain plants grow faster when exposed to specific frequencies of sound, while others show increased resistance to pests when subjected to low-frequency vibrations. These findings challenge the assumption that plants are entirely unresponsive to sound and open new avenues for understanding the full range of plant perception.

The mechanisms underlying plant sensitivity are still being explored, but scientists have identified several key components that contribute to these responses. One of the primary methods of detection involves the release of signaling molecules, such as calcium ions and reactive oxygen species, which act as internal messengers to coordinate cellular activity. These signals can travel through the plant's vascular system, triggering changes in gene expression, enzyme activity, and structural modifications. Additionally, the presence of specialized receptors on plant cell surfaces allows them to detect and interpret external stimuli, initiating appropriate physiological responses.

Understanding how plants detect and respond to their environment is not only fascinating from a scientific perspective but also has practical implications for agriculture and ecological conservation. By studying the ways in which plants perceive and react to their surroundings, researchers can develop more effective strategies for improving crop resilience, optimizing plant growth, and enhancing ecosystem stability. Furthermore, this knowledge can inform the development of bioengineered plants that are better adapted to environmental stressors, contributing to more sustainable agricultural practices.

As our understanding of plant sensitivity continues to evolve, it becomes increasingly clear that plants are not passive entities but rather active participants in their environments. Their ability to detect and respond to a wide range of stimuli demonstrates a level of complexity and adaptability that challenges traditional notions of plant life. By recognizing the intricate ways in which plants interact with their surroundings, we gain a deeper appreciation for the dynamic and interconnected nature of the natural world.

Sound and Plant Growth

Recent studies have shed light on the intriguing relationship between sound and plant growth, revealing that plants may respond to specific frequencies and vibrations in ways that influence their development. While plants do not possess auditory organs like humans or animals, research has shown that they can detect and react to sound waves, suggesting that they may have an indirect form of hearing. This discovery has sparked interest among scientists, who are exploring how sound exposure might affect plant physiology, nutrient uptake, and overall health.

One of the most notable areas of research involves the impact of music on plant growth. Several experiments have demonstrated that plants exposed to certain types of music—particularly classical compositions—exhibit enhanced growth rates compared to those in silent environments. A study conducted by researchers at the University of California found that tomato plants grown in the presence of classical music showed increased biomass and improved root development. Similarly, a 2014 study published in the *Journal of Agricultural Science* reported that plants exposed to soft instrumental music had higher levels of chlorophyll, indicating better photosynthetic efficiency. These findings suggest that sound may stimulate plant growth by promoting cellular activity and enhancing metabolic processes.

In addition to music, researchers have investigated the effects of white noise and ambient sounds on plant development. White noise, which consists of a broad spectrum of frequencies, has been shown to have a calming effect on plants, reducing stress and promoting healthier growth. A 2017 study published in *Plant Physiology and Biochemistry* found that plants exposed to continuous low-frequency white noise exhibited increased root elongation and improved nutrient absorption. This suggests that sound may play a role in regulating plant behavior, possibly by influencing the movement of water and nutrients within the plant's vascular system.

Another area of research focuses on the effects of vibrations on plant growth. Studies have shown that plants can detect and respond to mechanical vibrations, which can influence their development in various ways. For example, a 2019 study published in *Frontiers in Plant Science* found that exposing plants to low-frequency vibrations led to increased stem thickness and stronger root structures. Researchers believe that these vibrations may stimulate the production of plant hormones, such as auxins, which are responsible for regulating growth and development. This finding has important implications for agriculture, as it suggests that controlled vibrations could be used to enhance plant resilience and improve crop yields.

The effects of sound on plant growth are not limited to laboratory settings; field studies have also provided evidence of its impact. In agricultural contexts, farmers have experimented with using sound-based techniques to improve crop productivity. For instance, some vineyards have implemented sound-emitting devices that emit specific frequencies designed to deter pests and promote healthy plant growth. These devices work by creating an environment that is less favorable for harmful insects while encouraging beneficial ones, demonstrating the potential for sound to be used as a tool in sustainable farming practices.

Despite these promising findings, the exact mechanisms by which sound influences plant growth remain unclear. Scientists continue to investigate the role of sound in plant physiology, exploring how different frequencies and intensities affect cellular processes. Some researchers believe that sound may influence the movement of ions across cell membranes, affecting the flow of nutrients and water within the plant. Others suggest that sound waves may activate specific genes that regulate growth and stress responses. As research progresses, a more comprehensive understanding of the relationship between sound and plant development is likely to emerge.

The growing body of evidence supporting the impact of sound on plant growth has significant implications for both scientific research and practical applications. By understanding how plants respond to sound, scientists can develop new strategies for improving crop resilience, enhancing plant health, and promoting sustainable agricultural practices. Additionally, this knowledge may lead to the development of innovative technologies that utilize sound to support plant growth in controlled environments, such as greenhouses and vertical farms.

Farming Up:
A New Way to Grow

Traditional Farm
Large amounts

A Smarter Way to Grow

Vertical Farm
Grows crops indoors

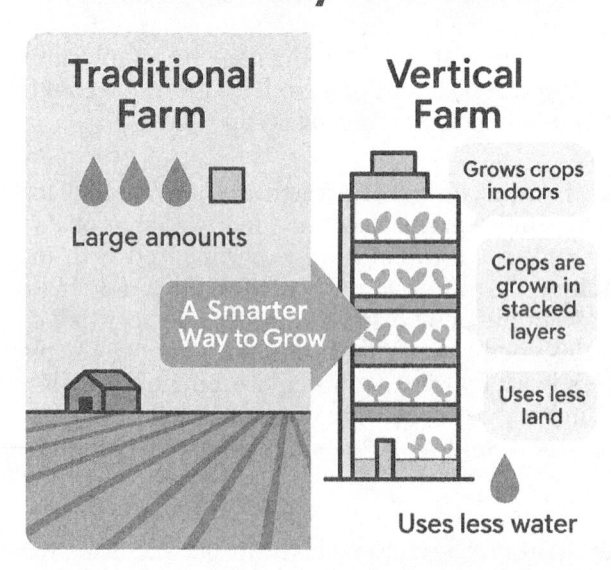

Crops are grown in stacked layers

Uses less land

Uses less water

Fig. 6 Traditional versus Vertical Farm (Source: Lexicon Labs)

As research into plant sensitivity to sound continues to expand, it becomes increasingly clear that plants are not merely passive organisms but are actively engaged with their environment in ways that are still being uncovered. The effects of sound on plant growth highlight the complexity of plant life and underscore the importance of further exploration into the ways in which plants perceive and respond to their surroundings. By continuing to study these interactions, we can gain valuable insights into the hidden world of plant communication and develop more effective strategies for cultivating healthy, thriving ecosystems.

Roots and Vibration

While much of the research on plant sensitivity has focused on their responses to light, temperature, and sound, another fascinating area of study involves their ability to detect and respond to vibrations. Unlike animals, which rely on ears and nervous systems to perceive sound, plants lack dedicated auditory organs. However, studies have shown that plants can sense and react to mechanical vibrations, suggesting that they may have an alternative way of perceiving their environment. This ability is particularly evident in the roots, where vibrations can influence growth patterns, nutrient uptake, and overall plant health.

RESEARCH FOCUS

Breakthrough Study on Plant Root Recognition and Kin Selection

In a 2007 study published in *Nature*, researchers Harsh Bais and Susan Dudley showed that the plant species *Cakile edentula* (sea rocket) can distinguish between the roots of its own siblings and those of unrelated plants. When grown next to kin, the plants restrained root growth, but when next to strangers, they aggressively expanded their root systems to compete for nutrients. This finding provided clear evidence that plants engage in kin recognition and adjust their growth behavior accordingly—indicating a level of social awareness previously unrecognized in flora. The study transformed our understanding of plant behavior below ground and introduced the concept of cooperative strategy among related plants.

Roots are highly sensitive to mechanical stimuli, and their ability to detect vibrations plays a crucial role in their function. When a plant's roots come into contact with soil particles, water, or other objects, they can sense the resulting vibrations and adjust their growth accordingly. This process, known as thigmoresponse, allows roots to navigate their environment and avoid obstacles, ensuring efficient nutrient absorption and water uptake. For example, if a root encounters a hard surface, it may change direction to find a path with more favorable conditions, demonstrating a form of mechanical responsiveness that is essential for survival.

Research has also shown that plants can detect vibrations caused by external forces, such as wind, animal movement, or even human activity. A 2018 study published in *Plant Signaling & Behavior* found that plants exposed to consistent vibrations exhibited changes in root architecture, with some species showing increased root branching and elongation. These responses suggest that plants can use vibration detection as a means of assessing their surroundings and adjusting their growth strategies accordingly. This ability may be particularly useful in environments where soil conditions are unpredictable, allowing plants to optimize their resource acquisition based on mechanical cues.

In addition to detecting vibrations from external sources, plants may also generate their own vibrational signals. Some researchers have proposed that plants use vibrations as a form of communication, transmitting information through the soil to neighboring plants. This hypothesis is supported by observations of plants responding to vibrations in ways that suggest a form of interaction. For instance, when one plant is disturbed, nearby plants may exhibit changes in growth or defense mechanisms, indicating that they are receiving and interpreting mechanical signals. This form of communication, though not yet fully understood, highlights the complexity of plant interactions and the potential for vibrational signaling to play a role in ecological networks.

The mechanisms behind vibration detection in plants are still being explored, but scientists have identified several possible pathways. One theory suggests that plants use mechanosensitive ion channels embedded in their cell membranes to detect mechanical stimuli. These channels open in response to pressure or movement, triggering a cascade of biochemical reactions that influence plant behavior. Another possibility is that plants rely on the movement of water and nutrients within their vascular system to transmit vibrational signals, similar to how sound travels through air. Regardless of the exact mechanism, the ability of plants to sense and respond to vibrations underscores their adaptability and the intricate ways in which they interact with their environment.

The study of vibration detection in plants has important implications for both ecological research and agricultural practices. Understanding how plants respond to mechanical stimuli can help scientists develop more effective strategies for managing plant growth in different environments. For example, farmers may use controlled vibrations to encourage root development in crops, improving their ability to absorb nutrients and resist drought. Additionally, this knowledge could be applied to the development of bioengineered plants that are better adapted to challenging conditions, such as compacted soils or unstable substrates.

As research into plant sensitivity continues to advance, the role of vibration detection in plant behavior is becoming increasingly clear. While plants may not hear in the same way as animals, their ability to sense and respond to mechanical stimuli reveals a level of awareness that challenges traditional assumptions about plant life. By studying these interactions, scientists can gain a deeper understanding of the complex relationships that exist within ecosystems and develop more sustainable approaches to plant cultivation and environmental management. This ongoing exploration of plant sensitivity highlights the remarkable adaptability of life and the many ways in which organisms interact with their surroundings.

The Mystery of Plant Perception

Despite the growing body of research on plant sensitivity, many questions remain about how plants perceive and respond to their environment. While scientists have identified several mechanisms that allow plants to detect and react to external stimuli, the full extent of their perceptual abilities is still not fully understood. This uncertainty has led to ongoing debates among researchers, with some arguing that plants possess a form of intelligence and others maintaining that their responses are purely reflexive and based on pre-programmed biological processes.

One of the central questions in this field is whether plants can truly "perceive" their environment in a way that resembles consciousness. Unlike animals, which have centralized nervous systems and brains that process sensory information, plants lack a similar structure. Instead, they rely on a decentralized network of cells and tissues that communicate through chemical and electrical signals. This difference in biological organization raises the question of whether plants experience their environment in a conscious or intentional way, or if their responses are simply the result of evolutionary adaptations that have developed over millions of years.

Some researchers propose that plants may have a form of distributed intelligence, where their ability to sense and respond to stimuli is spread throughout their entire structure rather than being localized in a single organ. This idea is supported by studies showing that plants can remember past experiences, such as exposure to drought or herbivory, and adjust their behavior accordingly. For example, some plants have been observed to produce defensive compounds more quickly when exposed to the same threat multiple times, suggesting a form of learning or adaptation. However, these responses are typically short-term and based on physiological changes rather than cognitive processing, making it difficult to classify them as true memory or intelligence.

Another area of debate centers on the role of plant perception in ecological interactions. If plants are capable of detecting and responding to their environment in complex ways, how does this affect their relationships with other organisms? Some scientists argue that plant perception plays a critical role in shaping ecosystems, influencing everything from pollination patterns to predator-prey dynamics. For instance, the ability of plants to detect and respond to vibrations may help them avoid damage from herbivores, while their chemical signaling capabilities allow them to warn neighboring plants of potential threats. These interactions suggest that plants are not passive elements in their environment but active participants in a dynamic and interconnected system.

Despite these insights, there is still much to learn about the limits of plant perception. While scientists have made significant progress in understanding how plants detect and respond to external stimuli, the question of whether they experience their environment in a meaningful or conscious way remains unanswered. This uncertainty highlights the need for further research, as well as a willingness to reconsider traditional assumptions about the nature of plant life.

As the field of plant science continues to evolve, so too does our understanding of the ways in which plants interact with their surroundings. By exploring the mysteries of plant perception, we gain a deeper appreciation for the complexity of life and the many ways in which organisms adapt to their environments. Whether or not plants possess a form of intelligence, their ability to sense and respond to their surroundings is a testament to the remarkable adaptability of life on Earth.

Did You Know?

Plants "see" light colors—using proteins like phytochromes and cryptochromes, plants distinguish red, blue, and ultraviolet light to time their growth and sleep cycles.

Roots dodge rocks—plant roots can sense vibrations and mechanical resistance in soil, rerouting growth to avoid obstacles before hitting them.

Plants may "hear" pollinators—some flowers increase nectar sweetness within minutes of detecting the wingbeat frequency of nearby bees.

Silent music, real results—low-frequency sound and white noise have been shown to boost chlorophyll content and nutrient uptake in tomatoes and spinach.

Venus flytraps remember touches—they only close after two signals within ~20 seconds, a simple form of memory that avoids false alarms.

Chapter 4

The Social Lives of Plants

Cooperation and Support

The idea that plants are passive, isolated organisms has been largely debunked by modern scientific research. In reality, plants form intricate networks of cooperation and support, particularly within forest ecosystems where they rely on one another for survival. This cooperative behavior challenges the traditional view of competition as the primary force shaping plant life, revealing instead a more nuanced and interconnected system in which plants work together to enhance their collective resilience. One of the most striking examples of this is the concept of "mother trees," which play a crucial role in nurturing younger plants and maintaining the health of the entire forest.

Mother trees are large, mature trees that act as central hubs within the mycorrhizal network, facilitating the exchange of nutrients and chemical signals among neighboring plants. These trees are often the oldest and most established members of a forest, and their extensive root systems allow them to connect with a wide range of other species. Through the fungal network, mother trees can supply younger trees with essential resources such as sugars, water, and minerals, helping them grow and develop more effectively. This form of intergenerational support ensures that even in challenging conditions, new growth can thrive, reinforcing the long-term stability of the ecosystem.

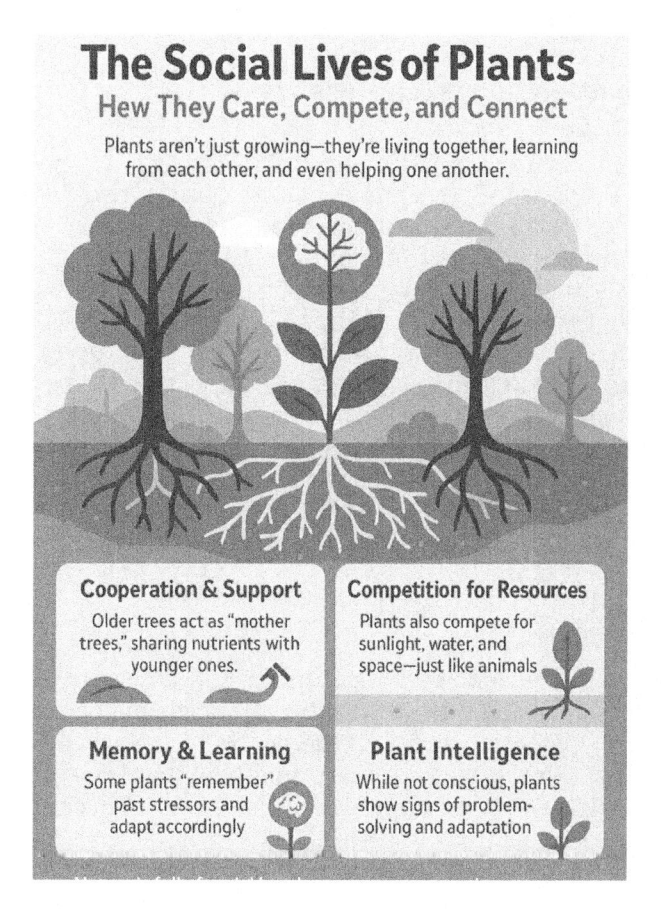

Fig. 7 The Social Lives of Plants (Source: Lexicon Labs)

Research conducted by ecologist Suzanne Simard and her team has provided compelling evidence for the existence of these cooperative relationships. Their studies have shown that trees in a forest are not merely competing for resources but are actively supporting each other through the underground fungal network. For example, in a study of Douglas fir and birch trees, Simard found that when one tree was under stress, it could send excess sugars to nearby trees, allowing them to survive and grow stronger. This kind of resource sharing suggests that forests are not just collections of individual trees but are instead complex, interdependent systems where the well-being of one tree directly impacts the health of others.

> **RESEARCH FOCUS**
>
> *Mimosa pudica* and Plant Memory
>
> In a 2014 study published in *Oecologia*, researcher Monica Gagliano demonstrated that the sensitive plant *Mimosa pudica* could learn from experience and retain that learning over time. By repeatedly dropping the plants without harming them, Gagliano observed that *Mimosa* stopped folding its leaves in response—indicating it had learned the drop was not a threat. Remarkably, this memory persisted for up to 28 days without reinforcement. The study was one of the first to show that plants are capable of a form of non-neural learning, challenging the belief that memory requires a brain. It sparked a major re-evaluation of plant cognition and sparked debate about the boundaries of intelligence in living organisms.

In addition to nutrient exchange, mother trees also play a role in communication, using the fungal network to transmit chemical signals that warn of potential threats. When a tree is attacked by pests or pathogens, it can release specific compounds that travel through the network, alerting neighboring trees to the danger. This early warning system allows other trees to activate their own defense mechanisms, such as producing toxic compounds or strengthening their cell walls. By working together in this way, plants can respond more effectively to environmental stressors, increasing their chances of survival and reducing the overall impact of disease or herbivory on the forest.

The concept of mother trees and their supportive role within the forest has significant implications for our understanding of plant life. It challenges the long-held assumption that plants are primarily competitive and highlights the importance of cooperation in maintaining ecological balance. This shift in perspective has important consequences for conservation efforts, as it underscores the need to protect not only individual species but also the complex networks that sustain them. By preserving the integrity of these underground connections, we can help ensure the long-term health and resilience of forest ecosystems.

Beyond the natural world, the lessons learned from these cooperative interactions have practical applications in agriculture and land management. Traditional farming practices often focus on maximizing yield through intensive cultivation, but this approach can disrupt the natural relationships between plants and fungi, leading to soil degradation and reduced biodiversity. By adopting more sustainable methods that encourage the development of healthy mycorrhizal networks, farmers can improve soil fertility, increase crop resilience, and reduce the need for synthetic fertilizers. Techniques such as cover cropping, reduced tillage, and the use of organic amendments can help maintain these beneficial relationships, promoting a more balanced and productive agricultural system.

The cooperative nature of plant life also raises interesting questions about the broader implications of these interactions. If plants are capable of supporting one another in such a sophisticated manner, what does this say about the nature of life itself? This line of inquiry has led some scientists to explore the possibility that plants possess a form of intelligence, albeit one that is fundamentally different from that of animals. While plants do not have brains or nervous systems, their ability to communicate, share resources, and adapt to their surroundings suggests that they are far more than simple organisms. Instead, they are active participants in a dynamic and interconnected web of life, constantly responding to and influencing their surroundings.

As our understanding of plant cooperation continues to evolve, it becomes increasingly clear that the natural world is far more complex and interconnected than we once believed. The discovery of mother trees and their role in fostering community among plants has reshaped our perception of forest ecosystems, revealing them as not just collections of individual organisms but as thriving, cooperative networks. This insight not only deepens our appreciation for the complexity of life but also highlights the importance of protecting and preserving these vital relationships. By recognizing the value of plant cooperation, we can take meaningful steps toward creating more sustainable and resilient ecosystems for future generations.

DR. LEO LEXICON

The Struggle for Survival

While cooperation and support are essential aspects of plant life, competition is equally fundamental to the survival and development of plant communities. Just as animals must compete for food, shelter, and mates, plants engage in a constant struggle for sunlight, water, and nutrients, often at the expense of their neighbors. This competition shapes the structure of ecosystems, influences the distribution of plant species, and drives the evolutionary adaptations that allow certain plants to thrive in specific environments. Understanding the dynamics of plant competition provides valuable insights into how forests, grasslands, and other plant-dominated landscapes function and how they respond to environmental changes.

One of the most obvious forms of plant competition occurs for access to sunlight, which is essential for photosynthesis. In dense forests, taller trees dominate the canopy, capturing the majority of available light while shading the understory. This creates a hierarchical structure in which only the most vigorous plants can reach the upper layers, while shorter or less competitive species are forced to adapt to lower light conditions. Some plants, such as shade-tolerant ferns and mosses, have evolved specialized strategies to survive in low-light environments, including slower growth rates and efficient nutrient absorption. Others, like climbing vines, use structural adaptations to reach higher elevations, often at the expense of the trees they climb. This interplay between competition and adaptation plays a crucial role in shaping the diversity and resilience of plant communities.

Water and soil nutrients are also key resources that drive plant competition. In arid environments, where water is scarce, plants have developed various strategies to maximize their access to this vital resource. Some species, such as cacti, store water in their tissues, while others, like desert shrubs, have deep root systems that tap into underground water sources. In more temperate regions, competition for nutrients can be just as intense, especially in nutrient-poor soils. Certain plants, such as legumes, form symbiotic relationships with nitrogen-fixing bacteria, allowing them to convert atmospheric nitrogen into a usable form. This advantage enables them to outcompete other species in nutrient-deficient environments, demonstrating how biological interactions can influence the outcome of competition.

Competition is not limited to above-ground interactions; it also extends beneath the soil, where roots vie for space and resources. In dense plant communities, roots must constantly adjust their architecture to optimize resource acquisition. Some species, such as grasses, develop extensive root systems that spread horizontally, allowing them to capture surface moisture and nutrients efficiently. Others, like trees, invest in deep roots that access water from deeper soil layers, reducing direct competition with shallow-rooted plants. This spatial partitioning of resources helps minimize conflict and allows multiple species to coexist within the same environment.

In addition to physical competition, plants also engage in chemical warfare to gain an advantage over their neighbors. Some species release allelopathic compounds—chemical substances that inhibit the growth of other plants—through their roots or leaves. A well-known example is the black walnut tree (Juglans nigra), which secretes juglone, a compound that suppresses the growth of many surrounding plants. This strategy allows the black walnut to dominate its immediate environment, reducing competition for resources. Similarly, certain grasses and shrubs produce chemicals that prevent the germination of seeds from other species, ensuring that they remain the dominant vegetation in their habitat.

Despite the apparent hostility of competition, it is a necessary and natural part of plant life. Without competition, ecosystems would lack the diversity and resilience needed to withstand environmental changes. The constant struggle for resources drives evolution, encouraging plants to develop more efficient ways of surviving and reproducing. This process not only shapes the characteristics of individual species but also contributes to the overall stability of ecosystems by preventing any single species from becoming too dominant.

Understanding plant competition is essential for both ecological research and practical applications in agriculture and land management. In natural ecosystems, competition helps regulate plant populations and maintain biodiversity, ensuring that no single species monopolizes the available resources. In agricultural settings, however, competition can be both a challenge and an opportunity. Farmers must carefully manage plant spacing, nutrient availability, and weed control to optimize crop yields while minimizing competition between different species. Techniques such as intercropping, where multiple plant species are grown together, can be used to create complementary relationships that reduce competition and enhance productivity.

The study of plant competition also has broader implications for conservation and environmental policy. As human activities continue to alter natural habitats, understanding how plants interact with one another becomes increasingly important. Protecting native plant species and restoring degraded ecosystems require a deep knowledge of the competitive dynamics that shape plant communities. By recognizing the role of competition in maintaining ecological balance, we can develop more effective strategies for preserving biodiversity and promoting the long-term health of our planet's ecosystems.

Ultimately, competition is an integral part of the plant world, driving the evolution of diverse strategies for survival and resource acquisition. While it may seem harsh, this process is essential for maintaining the balance and resilience of ecosystems. By studying how plants compete for resources, we gain valuable insights into the complexities of life and the intricate relationships that sustain the natural world. As our understanding of plant competition continues to grow, so too does our appreciation for the remarkable adaptability and resilience of plant life.

Memory and Learning in Plants

Plants may not have brains or nervous systems, but they are capable of adapting to their environment in ways that suggest a form of memory and learning. This ability is particularly evident in how plants respond to repeated stressors, such as drought, disease, or herbivory. Unlike animals, which can learn from experience through complex neural processes, plants rely on biochemical and physiological changes to retain information about past environmental conditions. These adaptations allow them to adjust their growth patterns, enhance their defenses, and improve their chances of survival under changing circumstances.

One of the most well-documented examples of plant memory is the way certain species respond to repeated exposure to environmental stress. For instance, when a plant experiences a period of drought, it undergoes a series of physiological changes, such as closing its stomata to reduce water loss and increasing root depth to access deeper soil moisture. If the same plant encounters another drought in the future, it often responds more quickly and effectively than it did during the first occurrence. This suggests that plants can "remember" past stress events and use this information to better prepare for similar challenges in the future. This phenomenon, known as "priming," is a form of adaptive memory that allows plants to anticipate and respond to environmental changes more efficiently.

The mechanisms behind plant memory are still being studied, but scientists believe that it involves changes in gene expression and the accumulation of specific chemical compounds. When a plant is exposed to a stressor, it activates certain genes that help it cope with the challenge. These genes may remain active even after the stressor has passed, allowing the plant to maintain a heightened state of readiness. Additionally, some research suggests that plants can store information about past stress events in the form of epigenetic modifications—changes in gene activity that do not alter the DNA sequence itself but can influence how genes are expressed over time. This means that a plant's response to a particular stressor can be influenced by the experiences of its ancestors, further reinforcing the idea that plants possess a form of inherited memory.

Another fascinating aspect of plant adaptation is their ability to modify their behavior in response to repeated stimuli. For example, some plants have been observed to grow toward light sources more efficiently after multiple exposures, suggesting that they can "learn" to optimize their growth strategies. Similarly, certain species of grasses have shown improved resistance to grazing after repeated herbivore attacks, indicating that they can adjust their defensive mechanisms based on past experiences. These responses are not random but rather highly coordinated, involving complex signaling pathways that enable plants to fine-tune their reactions to environmental cues.

The role of memory in plant development is also evident in the way seedlings respond to their surroundings. Young plants must navigate a complex and often unpredictable environment, making decisions about where to grow, how to allocate resources, and when to initiate flowering. Research has shown that seedlings can "remember" the direction of light, water, and nutrients, using this information to guide their growth patterns. This ability to retain and act upon environmental information is crucial for their survival, especially in competitive or resource-limited environments.

In addition to responding to external stressors, plants also exhibit forms of memory that are related to their internal biological rhythms. Many plants have an internal clock, or circadian rhythm, that helps them regulate processes such as photosynthesis, leaf movement, and flowering. This internal timing mechanism is influenced by environmental factors like light and temperature, but it also appears to be shaped by past experiences. Some studies have suggested that plants can adjust their circadian rhythms based on previous exposure to different light cycles, demonstrating a form of temporal memory that allows them to anticipate and adapt to changes in their environment.

The implications of plant memory extend beyond individual survival and into broader ecological and agricultural contexts. Understanding how plants retain and use information about past environmental conditions can help scientists develop more resilient crop varieties that are better adapted to climate change and other environmental stresses. By selecting for plants that exhibit strong memory responses, farmers and researchers can create more sustainable agricultural systems that require fewer inputs and are less vulnerable to extreme weather events.

Moreover, the study of plant memory has sparked new questions about the nature of intelligence and learning in non-animal organisms. While plants do not process information in the same way as humans or animals, their ability to sense, respond to, and remember past experiences suggests that they possess a form of distributed intelligence. This line of inquiry has led some scientists to propose that plants have a form of distributed intelligence, where their ability to sense, respond, and remember is spread throughout their entire structure rather than centralized in a single organ.

As research into plant memory continues to advance, it becomes increasingly clear that plants are far more complex and adaptable than previously thought. Their ability to retain information about past experiences and use it to improve their survival and growth is a testament to the remarkable resilience of life. By studying these processes, we gain valuable insights into the ways in which organisms interact with their environments and develop strategies for coping with change. This knowledge not only deepens our understanding of plant biology but also has important implications for agriculture, conservation, and the broader study of life on Earth.

Intelligence Without a Brain

For centuries, the scientific community has largely viewed plants as passive organisms, incapable of complex behaviors or decision-making. However, recent research has challenged this long-held assumption, revealing that plants possess a form of intelligence that, while fundamentally different from that of animals, is no less sophisticated. This new perspective is reshaping our understanding of plant life, prompting scientists to reconsider what it means to be intelligent and how different organisms perceive and interact with their environments.

At the heart of this shift is the recognition that intelligence is not solely defined by the presence of a brain or nervous system. Instead, it can manifest in various forms, depending on the organism's needs and evolutionary history. Plants, despite lacking neurons and synapses, have developed intricate mechanisms for sensing, responding to, and adapting to their environments. These capabilities suggest that intelligence is not limited to animals but is a broader, more inclusive concept that encompasses a wide range of life forms.

One of the most compelling arguments for plant intelligence comes from their ability to process and respond to environmental signals in a structured and purposeful way. Plants continuously monitor their surroundings, detecting changes in light, temperature, moisture, and even the presence of other organisms. They use this information to make decisions about where to grow, how to allocate resources, and when to initiate flowering. These responses are not random but are instead guided by complex biochemical and physiological processes that allow plants to optimize their survival and growth.

The concept of plant intelligence is further supported by their capacity for learning and adaptation. As discussed earlier, plants can "remember" past experiences and use this information to improve their responses to future challenges. This form of memory, though not stored in a central nervous system, is deeply embedded in their genetic and metabolic processes. By adjusting their responses to recurring environmental challenges, plants demonstrate a level of adaptability that is essential for thriving in dynamic ecosystems.

Another key aspect of plant intelligence is their ability to communicate and cooperate with other organisms. Through chemical signaling, mycorrhizal networks, and other forms of interaction, plants engage in a rich web of communication that facilitates resource sharing, defense, and mutual support. This interconnectedness suggests that plants are not isolated entities but rather active participants in a larger, cooperative system. Their ability to work together to enhance their collective survival challenges the notion that intelligence is inherently solitary or individualistic.

The debate over whether plants possess intelligence has sparked discussions among scientists, philosophers, and ecologists. Some argue that intelligence requires conscious awareness, a trait that plants do not possess. Others contend that intelligence should be understood in terms of functionality and adaptability, regardless of the underlying biological mechanisms. This ongoing dialogue highlights the complexity of defining intelligence and underscores the need for a more inclusive and nuanced approach to understanding the diverse ways in which organisms interact with their environments.

Beyond the scientific realm, the new view of plant intelligence has profound implications for how we perceive and interact with the natural world. If plants are indeed capable of sensing, learning, and adapting, then our relationship with them must be reevaluated. This realization calls for a more respectful and mindful approach to environmental stewardship, emphasizing the importance of preserving and protecting the intricate networks that sustain plant life. It also encourages us to recognize the value of all living organisms, regardless of their perceived complexity or similarity to human intelligence.

As research into plant intelligence continues to advance, it becomes increasingly clear that the natural world is far more complex and interconnected than we once believed. The discovery of plant memory, communication, and cooperation has expanded our understanding of life and highlighted the remarkable adaptability of organisms across the tree of life. By embracing this new perspective, we open the door to a deeper appreciation of the diversity and resilience of life on Earth. This shift in thinking not only enriches our scientific knowledge but also inspires a more holistic and compassionate approach to environmental conservation and sustainability.

Did You Know?

Trees share sugar with strangers—"mother trees" have been shown to nourish not just their seedlings, but also unrelated plants via underground fungal networks.

Plants have long-term memory—some plants respond more quickly to drought or pests if they have experienced the same stress in the past, a process called priming.

Plants use chemical sabotage—species like black walnut emit allelopathic chemicals that suppress nearby competitors, creating a biochemical exclusion zone.

Plant roots avoid each other—when related plants grow nearby, some root systems reduce overlap, possibly to prevent resource conflict—a hint at kin recognition.

Plants may inherit survival strategies—through epigenetic memory, offspring may "remember" environmental stress their parent experienced, altering how they grow.

Chapter 5

Applying Plant Communication

Regenerative Agriculture

Regenerative agriculture is an emerging farming approach that seeks to restore soil health, increase biodiversity, and improve ecosystem resilience by mimicking the natural processes found in healthy forests. Unlike conventional agricultural practices, which often deplete soil nutrients and disrupt ecological balance, regenerative methods emphasize the importance of maintaining and enhancing the underground networks that support plant life. These networks, particularly mycorrhizal fungi, play a critical role in nutrient cycling, water retention, and plant communication, making them essential components of sustainable farming systems.

One of the most significant benefits of regenerative agriculture is its ability to rebuild soil fertility without relying on synthetic fertilizers or chemical pesticides. By encouraging the growth of diverse plant species and fostering strong relationships between plants and beneficial microorganisms, farmers can create more resilient and productive ecosystems. Techniques such as cover cropping, reduced tillage, and composting help maintain and enhance these underground networks, allowing plants to share resources and communicate more effectively. This not only improves crop yields but also reduces the environmental impact of farming by minimizing the need for artificial inputs.

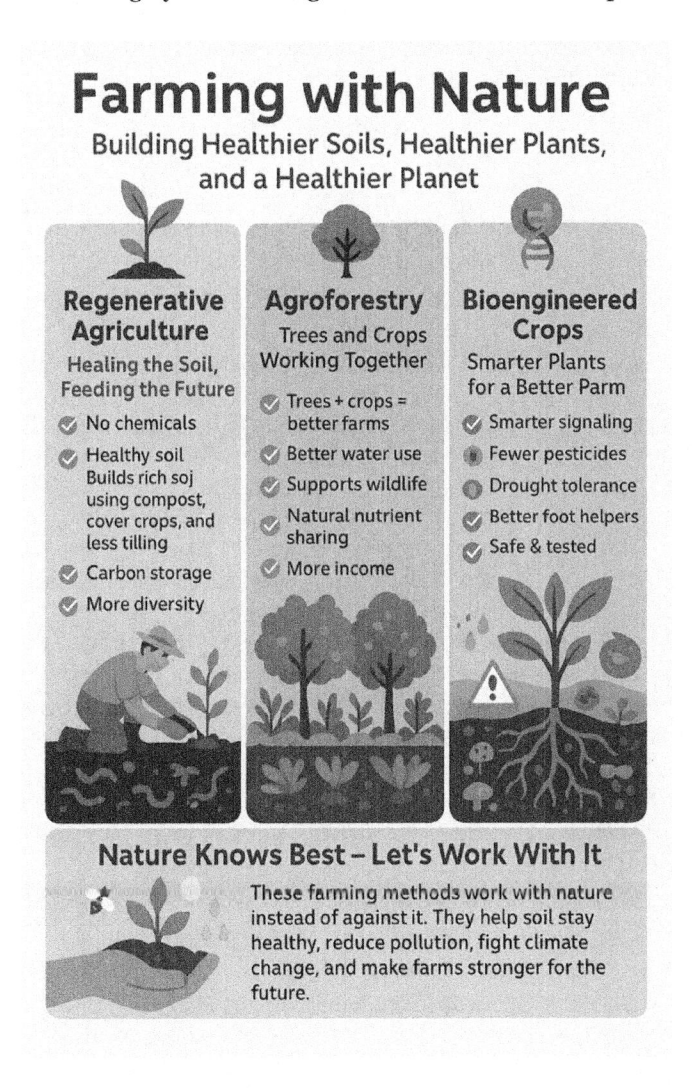

Farming with Nature
Building Healthier Soils, Healthier Plants, and a Healthier Planet

Regenerative Agriculture
Healing the Soil, Feeding the Future
- No chemicals
- Healthy soil Builds rich soj using compost, cover crops, and less tilling
- Carbon storage
- More diversity

Agroforestry
Trees and Crops Working Together
- Trees + crops = better farms
- Better water use
- Supports wildlife
- Natural nutrient sharing
- More income

Bioengineered Crops
Smarter Plants for a Better Parm
- Smarter signaling
- Fewer pesticides
- Drought tolerance
- Better foot helpers
- Safe & tested

Nature Knows Best – Let's Work With It
These farming methods work with nature instead of against it. They help soil stay healthy, reduce pollution, fight climate change, and make farms stronger for the future.

Fig. 8 Farming with Nature (Source: Lexicon Labs)

In addition to improving soil health, regenerative agriculture promotes carbon sequestration, helping to mitigate the effects of climate change.

Healthy soils rich in organic matter and microbial activity are capable of storing large amounts of carbon, reducing greenhouse gas emissions, and enhancing the overall stability of the environment. By adopting regenerative practices, farmers can contribute to global efforts to combat climate change while also ensuring long-term food security for future generations.

RESEARCH FOCUS

Regenerative Agriculture in the Loess Plateau, China

A landmark ecological restoration project on China's Loess Plateau offers compelling evidence of how regenerative agriculture can transform degraded land at scale. Starting in the late 1990s, the Chinese government, in collaboration with the World Bank, implemented large-scale regenerative practices—including terracing, controlled grazing, reforestation, and the use of cover crops. Over 20 years, these interventions restored over 35,000 square kilometers of eroded, desertified land. Soil organic matter increased significantly, water retention improved, crop yields doubled in some areas, and biodiversity rebounded. The success of the Loess Plateau project has been cited globally as proof that regenerative approaches not only heal soil but also uplift rural economies and restore ecological balance in some of the most fragile environments on Earth. The study was reported in Science in 2014.

Another key aspect of regenerative agriculture is its focus on biodiversity. Traditional monoculture farming systems, which rely on growing a single crop over large areas, often lead to soil degradation, pest outbreaks, and reduced resilience to environmental stressors. In contrast, regenerative farming encourages the cultivation of diverse plant species, creating a more balanced and self-sustaining ecosystem. This diversity not only supports a wider range of beneficial organisms, such as pollinators and soil microbes, but also enhances the ability of plants to communicate and cooperate through their underground networks.

The principles of regenerative agriculture are increasingly being adopted by farmers around the world, driven by a growing awareness of the limitations of industrial farming and the urgent need for sustainable food production. Organizations such as the Rodale Institute and the Savory Institute have been at the forefront of promoting regenerative practices, offering research, education, and support to farmers interested in transitioning to more ecologically sound methods. As more people recognize the value of working with nature rather than against it, regenerative agriculture is gaining momentum as a viable alternative to traditional farming systems.

By learning from the natural processes that sustain forests and other ecosystems, regenerative agriculture offers a promising path forward for food production. It highlights the importance of understanding and preserving the complex interactions that allow plants to thrive, demonstrating that sustainable farming is not only possible but also essential for the health of both the planet and its inhabitants.

Agroforestry: Integrating Trees and Crops

Agroforestry is a land management system that combines the cultivation of trees with crops or livestock, creating a more diverse and resilient agricultural landscape. This practice is inspired by the natural interactions observed in forests, where trees and understory plants coexist in a mutually beneficial relationship. By integrating trees into farmland, agroforestry mimics the functions of natural ecosystems, promoting biodiversity, improving soil health, and enhancing the overall productivity of the land.

One of the primary advantages of agroforestry is its ability to support plant communication and cooperation. Trees, especially those with extensive root systems, form symbiotic relationships with mycorrhizal fungi, enabling them to exchange nutrients and chemical signals with neighboring plants. This network allows for the transfer of resources, such as water and minerals, across different species, creating a more efficient and sustainable system. For example, in a mixed agroforestry system, fruit trees may provide shade and nutrients to smaller crops, while the crops in turn supply organic matter that enriches the soil and supports fungal growth.

Agroforestry also plays a crucial role in improving soil structure and water retention. Tree roots help prevent erosion, reduce soil compaction, and increase moisture retention, making the land more resistant to drought and other environmental stresses. The leaf litter produced by trees adds organic matter to the soil, further enhancing its fertility and supporting the growth of beneficial microorganisms. This natural process of nutrient cycling mirrors the way forests function, demonstrating how agroforestry can replicate the ecological benefits of natural ecosystems in agricultural settings.

In addition to its environmental benefits, agroforestry has economic and social advantages for farmers. By diversifying their income sources through the production of multiple crops and products—such as timber, fruits, nuts, and medicinal plants—farmers can become more financially stable and less vulnerable to market fluctuations. This diversification also helps reduce the risk of crop failure due to pests, diseases, or extreme weather events, making agroforestry a valuable strategy for climate resilience.

Moreover, agroforestry supports the development of more sustainable and equitable food systems. By incorporating trees into farming landscapes, agroforestry helps preserve native plant species and wildlife habitats, contributing to broader conservation efforts. It also aligns with the principles of permaculture, which emphasizes designing agricultural systems that mimic the patterns and relationships found in natural ecosystems. This holistic approach not only benefits the environment but also fosters a deeper connection between farmers and the land they cultivate.

The success of agroforestry depends on careful planning and implementation. Farmers must select tree species that are well-suited to their local climate and soil conditions, while also considering the needs of the crops or livestock they intend to grow alongside them. Proper spacing, pruning, and maintenance are essential to ensure that all elements of the system work together harmoniously. Despite these challenges, the long-term benefits of agroforestry make it a compelling option for farmers seeking to build more resilient and sustainable agricultural systems.

As interest in agroforestry continues to grow, governments, NGOs, and research institutions are investing in programs that support its adoption. These initiatives provide training, financial incentives, and technical assistance to farmers who want to transition to agroforestry practices. By promoting this approach, we can move toward a more sustainable and regenerative agricultural model that honors the interconnectedness of all living things.

Bioengineered Crops

Advances in biotechnology have opened new possibilities for enhancing plant communication and improving agricultural productivity. Bioengineered crops are designed to respond more effectively to environmental stressors, resist pests and diseases, and optimize resource use, all of which contribute to more sustainable and efficient farming systems. One of the most promising applications of bioengineering in agriculture is the enhancement of plant signaling pathways, allowing crops to communicate more effectively with each other and with the surrounding ecosystem.

A key area of research involves modifying plants to produce specific chemical signals that promote growth, defense, and nutrient uptake. For instance, scientists are exploring ways to enhance the release of volatile organic compounds (VOCs) that attract beneficial insects, deter pests, or signal nearby plants to prepare for potential threats. By engineering plants to emit these compounds more efficiently, researchers aim to reduce the reliance on synthetic pesticides and fertilizers, making farming more environmentally friendly and cost-effective.

Another exciting development in bioengineering is the improvement of root exudates, the chemical compounds released by plant roots into the soil. These exudates play a vital role in plant-microbe interactions, influencing the availability of nutrients and the health of the soil. Scientists are working to develop crops that release more beneficial exudates, which can encourage the growth of nitrogen-fixing bacteria, mycorrhizal fungi, and other microbes that support plant growth. This approach not only enhances crop productivity but also promotes soil health and reduces the need for chemical inputs.

In addition to improving nutrient uptake, bioengineered crops are being developed to better withstand environmental stressors such as drought, salinity, and extreme temperatures. By enhancing the genetic traits that enable plants to detect and respond to environmental cues, scientists are creating crops that are more resilient to changing climatic conditions. For example, some genetically modified plants have been engineered to produce higher levels of protective compounds that help them survive prolonged periods of water scarcity or exposure to harmful pathogens.

The use of bioengineering in agriculture also extends to the development of crops that can communicate more effectively with their surroundings. Researchers are exploring ways to modify plants so that they can detect and respond to changes in soil composition, temperature, and light more efficiently. This could lead to the creation of crops that are better adapted to their environments, reducing the need for intensive management and increasing overall farm efficiency.

Despite its potential, the use of bioengineered crops remains a topic of debate. While many scientists and farmers see it as a powerful tool for addressing food security and environmental challenges, others raise concerns about the long-term impacts of genetic modification on ecosystems and human health. As research in this field continues, it will be important to balance innovation with caution, ensuring that the benefits of bioengineering are realized without compromising the integrity of natural systems.

Overall, the integration of bioengineered crops into agricultural practices represents a significant step forward in our ability to work with nature rather than against it. By enhancing plant communication and resilience, these innovations have the potential to transform the way we grow food, making it more sustainable, productive, and aligned with the natural processes that sustain life on Earth.

Sustainable Farming

Sustainable farming is an essential component of modern agriculture, focusing on practices that maintain ecological balance, conserve natural resources, and support long-term food security. Unlike conventional farming, which often prioritizes short-term yield at the expense of environmental health, sustainable farming emphasizes the importance of working with natural systems rather than imposing control over them. This approach recognizes the intricate relationships between plants, soil, and the broader ecosystem, and seeks to strengthen these connections to create more resilient and productive agricultural landscapes.

One of the core principles of sustainable farming is the preservation and enhancement of soil health. Healthy soil is the foundation of any productive agricultural system, and sustainable practices such as crop rotation, composting, and reduced chemical inputs help maintain its fertility and structure. By avoiding the overuse of synthetic fertilizers and pesticides, farmers can reduce soil degradation and protect the delicate microbial communities that support plant growth. These practices also align with the natural communication networks that exist in the soil, allowing plants to interact more effectively with their environment.

Another key aspect of sustainable farming is the promotion of biodiversity. Monoculture farming, which involves growing a single crop over large areas, can lead to soil depletion, increased vulnerability to pests and diseases, and reduced resilience to climate change. In contrast, sustainable farming systems encourage the cultivation of a wide variety of plant species, creating a more balanced and self-sustaining environment. This diversity not only supports a greater range of beneficial organisms but also enhances the ability of plants to communicate and collaborate through their underground networks, leading to healthier and more productive farms.

Water conservation is another critical element of sustainable farming, particularly in regions facing increasing water scarcity due to climate change. Techniques such as drip irrigation, rainwater harvesting, and the use of drought-resistant crop varieties help reduce water usage while maintaining high yields. Additionally, the integration of cover crops and mulching helps retain soil moisture, reduce evaporation, and support the development of healthy root systems. These strategies not only benefit individual farms but also contribute to the broader goal of protecting water resources for future generations.

Sustainable farming also places a strong emphasis on reducing waste and maximizing resource efficiency. Practices such as integrated pest management, which uses natural predators and biological controls instead of chemical pesticides, help minimize environmental harm while maintaining crop health. Similarly, the use of renewable energy sources, such as solar-powered irrigation systems and wind turbines, reduces the carbon footprint of farming operations. These innovations demonstrate that sustainability and productivity are not mutually exclusive, but rather complementary goals that can be achieved through thoughtful and informed decision-making.

In addition to environmental benefits, sustainable farming has positive implications for rural communities and food systems. By reducing dependence on external inputs and fostering local food production, sustainable practices can empower farmers and strengthen food sovereignty. Small-scale farmers, in particular, can benefit from these approaches, as they often have limited access to expensive chemical inputs and are more vulnerable to the impacts of climate change. By adopting sustainable techniques, they can improve their livelihoods while protecting the land for future generations.

The shift toward sustainable farming is supported by a growing body of research and policy initiatives aimed at promoting more ecologically sound agricultural practices. Governments, non-profit organizations, and agricultural research institutions are investing in programs that provide education, funding, and technical assistance to farmers interested in transitioning to sustainable methods. These efforts reflect a broader recognition of the need to rethink how we grow food in a way that is both productive and responsible.

As the global population continues to grow and the demand for food increases, the importance of sustainable farming cannot be overstated. By embracing practices that align with the natural rhythms of the Earth, we can ensure that future generations will have access to healthy, abundant food while preserving the ecosystems that support life on our planet. Sustainable farming is not just a response to current challenges—it is a vision for a more resilient and equitable agricultural future.

Did You Know?

Some crops can be trained to 'whisper' for help—bioengineered plants are being developed to emit early VOC distress signals, drawing predators before pests cause visible damage.

Trees in agroforestry help crops thrive—in mixed farms, nitrogen-fixing trees like *Gliricidia sepium* boost maize yields by enriching soil and facilitating root-level communication.

Mycorrhizal fungi act as underground climate buffers— healthy fungal networks not only share water among plants but also improve drought resilience by up to 40% in some polyculture systems.

Plants can be engineered to release custom root exudates— new biotech allows crops to "invite" specific beneficial microbes, optimizing nutrient absorption and plant cooperation.

Cover crops talk underground—legumes used as off-season ground cover send chemical signals that improve the mycorrhizal readiness of cash crops planted months later.

Chapter 6

The Philosophy of Plant Life

Recognizing Plant Genius

For centuries, plants have always been viewed as passive entities—static, silent, and largely ignored in the grand narrative of life on Earth. This perception has shaped our understanding of the natural world, leading to a worldview that prioritizes animals and humans as the primary actors in ecological systems. However, the growing body of scientific research into plant communication, intelligence, and cooperation is challenging these long-held assumptions. As we come to understand that plants are not merely part of the environment but active participants in it, we must reconsider how we interact with them and what this means for our relationship with the natural world.

One of the most profound implications of this new perspective is the way it reshapes our ethical considerations. If plants are capable of sensing their surroundings, responding to threats, and even communicating with one another, does this change the way we treat them? Traditional views of plants as inert resources have led to widespread deforestation, habitat destruction, and agricultural practices that prioritize short-term gains over long-term sustainability.

But if we recognize that plants are more than just passive organisms, we may be compelled to adopt more thoughtful and respectful approaches to land use, conservation, and environmental stewardship.

This shift in perspective also has significant consequences for how we approach agriculture. For centuries, farming has relied heavily on chemical inputs such as synthetic fertilizers and pesticides, often at the expense of soil health and biodiversity. However, by understanding the intricate relationships between plants and their environment—including the role of mycorrhizal networks, chemical signaling, and root exudates—we can develop more sustainable and regenerative agricultural practices. Techniques such as cover cropping, reduced tillage, and the cultivation of diverse plant species can help maintain healthy soil ecosystems, reduce the need for artificial interventions, and promote long-term crop resilience.

RESEARCH FOCUS

The Swiss Federal Ethics Committee Report

In 2008, the Swiss Federal Ethics Committee on Non-Human Biotechnology published a groundbreaking report titled *The Dignity of Living Beings with Regard to Plants*. Commissioned as part of Switzerland's constitutional commitment to protecting the dignity of all living beings, the report asked whether plants should have moral standing independent of their utility to humans. While the committee stopped short of equating plant rights with animal rights, it concluded that "arbitrary harm" to plants—for example, decapitating flowers solely for amusement—could be considered ethically unjustifiable. This was the first official government-backed statement suggesting that plants possess intrinsic value and may deserve ethical consideration. The report sparked global debate, challenging Western anthropocentric views and highlighting the need to reconsider our philosophical and moral relationship with the vegetal world.

Beyond agriculture, the recognition of plant intelligence and communication has broader implications for environmental policy and conservation efforts. Forests, which have long been seen as collections of individual trees, are now understood as complex, interdependent networks where information flows continuously through underground fungal connections. This realization underscores the importance of protecting not only individual species but also the intricate relationships that sustain entire ecosystems. Conservation strategies that focus on preserving these networks rather than just protecting individual plants or animals may lead to more effective and holistic approaches to environmental preservation.

Moreover, the study of plant communication challenges the anthropocentric view that intelligence is a uniquely human trait. While plants do not possess brains or nervous systems in the traditional sense, their ability to perceive, respond to, and adapt to their environment suggests that intelligence takes many forms. This realization invites us to expand our understanding of what it means to be intelligent and to appreciate the diversity of life in all its complexity. It also raises important philosophical questions about the nature of consciousness, adaptation, and survival across different species.

As our understanding of plant communication continues to evolve, it becomes increasingly clear that our relationship with plants is far more nuanced than previously believed. By recognizing their capacity for communication, cooperation, and adaptation, we gain a deeper appreciation for the interconnectedness of life on Earth. This newfound understanding not only enriches our scientific knowledge but also calls for a more thoughtful and respectful approach to the natural world. In doing so, we take an important step toward fostering a more sustainable and harmonious relationship with the environment, one that acknowledges the vital role that plants play in sustaining life on our planet.

The Ethics of Plant Life

As our understanding of plant communication and intelligence deepens, it becomes increasingly difficult to ignore the ethical implications of how we treat these organisms. Traditionally, plants have been viewed as resources—tools to be used for food, medicine, and industrial purposes. This utilitarian perspective has justified large-scale deforestation, habitat destruction, and agricultural practices that prioritize short-term gains over long-term sustainability. However, if plants are capable of sensing their environment, responding to threats, and even communicating with one another, then the question arises: do they deserve a level of ethical consideration similar to that afforded to animals?

One of the central ethical concerns is the impact of human activities on plant life. Deforestation, for example, not only destroys habitats but also disrupts the vast underground networks that connect plant communities. When forests are cleared, the mycorrhizal fungi that facilitate nutrient exchange and communication among trees are often destroyed, leading to long-term ecological damage. Similarly, the widespread use of synthetic fertilizers and pesticides can harm not only target organisms but also the delicate balance of microbial and plant interactions that support ecosystem health. These practices raise serious ethical questions about whether we are respecting the intrinsic value of plant life or simply treating it as a means to an end.

Another ethical dilemma involves the use of genetically modified plants. While genetic engineering has the potential to improve crop yields, enhance resistance to pests, and address food security challenges, it also raises concerns about the unintended consequences of altering plant genetics. Some scientists argue that modifying plants to suit human needs may disrupt natural evolutionary processes and weaken the resilience of plant populations. Others warn that the commercialization of genetically modified crops could lead to the monopolization of seed supplies, limiting access for small-scale farmers and reducing biodiversity. These issues highlight the need for careful ethical deliberation when it comes to manipulating plant life for human benefit.

The ethical treatment of plants also extends to the way we interact with them in everyday life. Many people consume plant-based foods without considering the broader implications of their choices. While eating plants is generally considered more sustainable than consuming animal products, the methods used to cultivate and harvest them can still have significant environmental and ethical consequences. Industrial agriculture, for instance, often relies on intensive practices that degrade soil health, deplete water resources, and contribute to climate change. By making more conscious choices about how we grow, consume, and interact with plants, we can begin to align our actions with a more ethical and sustainable approach to food production.

Furthermore, the recognition of plant intelligence and communication challenges the assumption that plants are inherently less valuable than animals. If plants are capable of responding to their environment, adapting to stressors, and forming cooperative relationships, then they deserve a level of respect and protection similar to that afforded to other living beings. This perspective has already influenced some conservation efforts, with initiatives focused on preserving native plant species and restoring degraded ecosystems. However, much more needs to be done to ensure that plants are not treated as expendable resources but as integral components of the biosphere.

Ultimately, the ethical considerations surrounding plant life are complex and multifaceted. They require us to rethink our relationship with the natural world and consider the long-term consequences of our actions. By acknowledging the intelligence, sensitivity, and interconnectedness of plant life, we can move toward a more ethical and sustainable approach to environmental stewardship—one that recognizes the intrinsic value of all living organisms, regardless of their perceived complexity or utility.

The Human-Nature Connection

As our understanding of plant communication and intelligence expands, it becomes increasingly clear that our relationship with the natural world is more deeply intertwined than we once believed. Plants are not just background elements in our environment; they are active participants in a vast, dynamic network of interactions that shape the ecosystems we depend on. Recognizing this connection has profound implications for how we perceive and engage with the natural world, encouraging a more mindful and respectful approach to our surroundings.

One of the most significant ways in which this connection manifests is through the emotional and psychological benefits of interacting with plants. Studies have shown that spending time in natural environments, particularly around plants, can reduce stress, improve mood, and enhance overall well-being. This phenomenon, often referred to as "biophilia," suggests that humans have an innate affinity for the natural world, and that our mental and physical health is closely linked to our relationship with plants. Whether it's the calming presence of a houseplant, the therapeutic effects of gardening, or the restorative power of a forest walk, the human-nature connection plays a vital role in our lives.

In addition to its psychological benefits, this connection also has practical implications for how we manage and protect the environment. As we become more aware of the intricate relationships between plants, fungi, and other organisms, we are better equipped to make informed decisions about land use, conservation, and sustainability. For example, understanding the role of mycorrhizal networks in supporting plant growth can lead to more effective reforestation efforts, while recognizing the importance of plant communication can inspire new approaches to agriculture that work in harmony with natural systems rather than against them.

Moreover, the human-nature connection fosters a sense of responsibility and stewardship. When we see plants not as passive resources but as active participants in the web of life, we are more likely to take steps to protect and preserve them. This shift in perspective can lead to more sustainable practices, from planting native species in urban areas to supporting policies that prioritize ecological health. It also encourages individuals to reflect on their own impact on the environment and consider how their daily choices affect the natural world.

By deepening our connection with plants, we not only gain a greater appreciation for the complexity of life but also open the door to a more balanced and harmonious relationship with the Earth. This understanding reminds us that we are not separate from nature but an integral part of it, and that our well-being is inextricably linked to the health of the ecosystems that sustain us. As we continue to explore the hidden world of plant life, we are reminded of the importance of nurturing this connection and working toward a future in which both humans and plants can thrive together.

A New Way of Seeing

As our understanding of plant communication and intelligence continues to evolve, it becomes increasingly clear that the way we perceive and interact with the natural world must also change. No longer can we view plants as mere background elements or passive resources; instead, we must recognize them as active participants in a vast, interconnected system that sustains life on Earth. This shift in perspective not only deepens our scientific knowledge but also encourages a more thoughtful and respectful approach to the environment.

One of the most immediate consequences of this new understanding is the need to rethink our relationship with plants in everyday life. From the food we eat to the spaces we inhabit, our interactions with plants shape the world around us. By cultivating a deeper awareness of their roles in ecosystems, we can make more informed choices that support their health and well-being. For instance, choosing to grow native plants in our gardens, reducing the use of chemical pesticides, and supporting sustainable agricultural practices can all contribute to a more balanced and resilient environment.

In addition to individual actions, this new perspective also has broader implications for how we design and manage landscapes. Urban planning, for example, can incorporate more green spaces that foster plant diversity and support natural communication networks. By creating environments that allow plants to thrive, we not only enhance biodiversity but also improve air quality, regulate temperature, and provide essential habitats for wildlife. Similarly, reforestation efforts that prioritize the restoration of mycorrhizal networks can help rebuild degraded ecosystems and promote long-term ecological stability.

Perhaps most importantly, this shift in understanding encourages a more holistic and compassionate approach to environmental stewardship. If plants are capable of sensing their surroundings, responding to threats, and even cooperating with one another, then it follows that they deserve a level of respect and care similar to that given to other living beings. This realization challenges us to move beyond a purely utilitarian view of nature and embrace a more ethical and sustainable way of living. It reminds us that we are not separate from the natural world but deeply embedded within it, and that our well-being is inextricably linked to the health of the ecosystems that sustain us.

As we continue to explore the hidden language of plants, we are reminded of the importance of listening—not just to the words we speak, but to the subtle signals that the natural world sends us every day. By opening our eyes to the complexity of plant life, we take a crucial step toward fostering a more harmonious relationship with the Earth. This journey of discovery not only enriches our understanding of the world but also inspires us to live in a way that honors the intricate web of life that surrounds us.

Did You Know?

Some trees 'grieve' when neighbors die—research in Swiss forests shows older trees reduce nutrient flow through fungal links after the death of a nearby tree, suggesting selective disconnection behavior.

Plants recalibrate circadian rhythms after trauma—studies on Arabidopsis reveal that physical stress or prolonged shade can permanently shift their internal clocks to match new light cycles.

Fungal networks can detect species identity—mycorrhizal fungi modulate nutrient sharing based on whether connected plants are kin or strangers, exhibiting network-level preference.

Forest edges speak differently—plants on the periphery of forests release different blends of VOCs than interior trees, adapting to more frequent environmental stress and herbivory.

Spiritual traditions mirror ecological truths—Indigenous worldviews that see plants as "relatives" rather than "resources" align closely with scientific findings about plant interdependence and reciprocity.

Chapter 7

The Future of Plant Communication

Emerging Technologies

As our understanding of plant communication continues to expand, so too does the development of new technologies that allow scientists to study and interact with these complex systems in unprecedented ways. Advances in fields such as bioacoustics, chemical analysis, and artificial intelligence are opening up new avenues for research, enabling us to decode the hidden language of plants more effectively than ever before. These innovations not only deepen our scientific knowledge but also have practical applications in agriculture, conservation, and environmental monitoring.

One of the most promising areas of research is bioacoustics —the study of sound and its effects on plant life. While plants do not possess ears or vocal cords, they can detect and respond to vibrations and sound waves, suggesting that they may have a form of auditory perception. Researchers have used sensitive microphones and acoustic sensors to analyze the subtle sounds produced by plants, revealing that they may communicate through low-frequency vibrations. Some studies have even suggested that certain frequencies of sound can influence plant growth, leading to increased biomass and improved nutrient absorption. By developing more advanced listening devices and analyzing the acoustic signals emitted by plants, scientists hope to uncover new insights into how plants perceive and respond to their environment.

In addition to sound, researchers are using sophisticated chemical analysis techniques to study the volatile organic compounds (VOCs) that plants release. These compounds serve as chemical signals, allowing plants to warn each other of threats, attract pollinators, and regulate their own growth. High-performance liquid chromatography (HPLC) and gas chromatography-mass spectrometry (GC-MS) are among the tools being used to identify and quantify these chemical messages, providing valuable data on how plants interact with one another and their surroundings. As these analytical methods become more refined, they will enable scientists to better understand the complexity of plant signaling and develop strategies for enhancing plant resilience in agricultural and ecological contexts.

Artificial intelligence (AI) is also playing an increasingly important role in plant research. Machine learning algorithms are being used to analyze large datasets of plant behavior, identifying patterns and correlations that might be difficult for humans to detect. For example, AI models can predict how plants will respond to different environmental conditions based on historical data, helping farmers make more informed decisions about crop management. Additionally, AI-powered imaging technology is being used to monitor plant health in real time, detecting early signs of disease or stress before they become visible to the naked eye. These advancements are not only improving our ability to study plant communication but also paving the way for more efficient and sustainable agricultural practices.

Another exciting development is the use of sensor networks to monitor plant activity across large areas. These networks consist of small, wireless sensors that can measure a variety of environmental factors, including temperature, humidity, soil moisture, and light levels. By deploying these sensors in forests, farms, and urban green spaces, researchers can gather continuous data on how plants respond to changing conditions. This information can be used to track the health of ecosystems, assess the impact of climate change, and develop strategies for preserving biodiversity. In the future, these sensor networks could be integrated with AI systems to create smart environments that automatically adjust to the needs of the plants they support.

Emerging Technologies Revolutionizining the Science of Plants

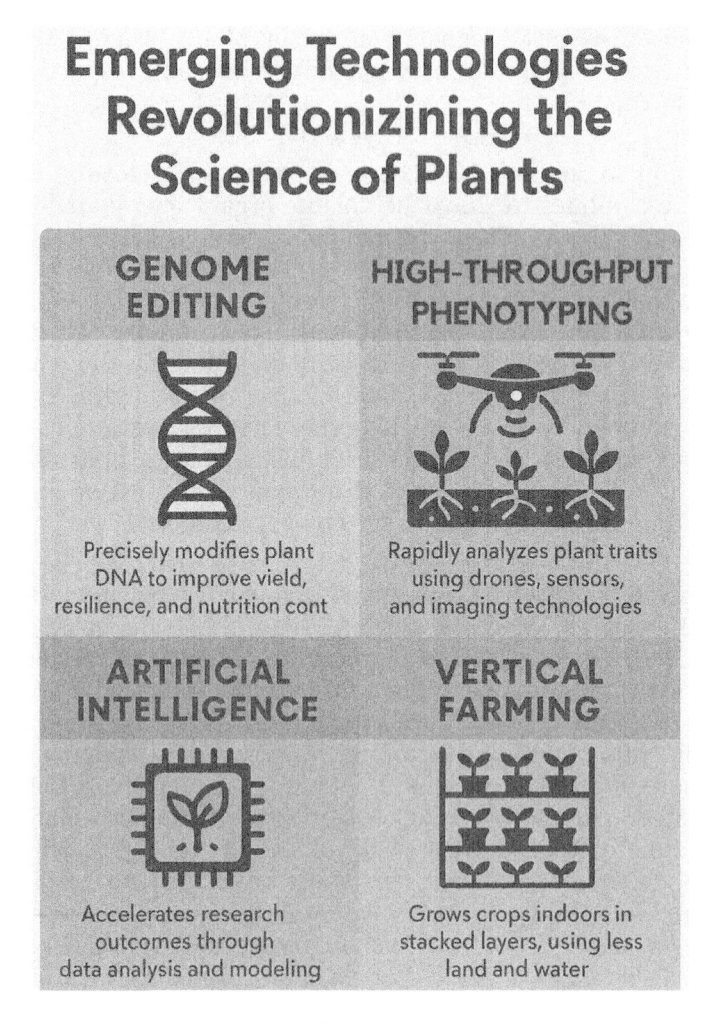

GENOME EDITING
Precisely modifies plant DNA to improve yield, resilience, and nutrition cont

HIGH-THROUGHPUT PHENOTYPING
Rapidly analyzes plant traits using drones, sensors, and imaging technologies

ARTIFICIAL INTELLIGENCE
Accelerates research outcomes through data analysis and modeling

VERTICAL FARMING
Grows crops indoors in stacked layers, using less land and water

Fig. 9 Emerging Technologies (Source: Lexicon Labs)

As these technologies continue to evolve, they are transforming the way we study and interact with plant life. By combining advances in bioacoustics, chemical analysis, and artificial intelligence, scientists are gaining a more comprehensive understanding of the complex communication systems that underpin plant survival. These innovations not only enhance our scientific knowledge but also offer practical solutions for addressing some of the most pressing challenges facing our planet, from food security to environmental conservation.

RESEARCH FOCUS

Decoding Plant Stress Signals Using AI and Bioacoustics

In a groundbreaking 2019 study published in *Cell*, researchers at Tel Aviv University led by Itzhak Khait and Lilach Hadany demonstrated that stressed plants emit ultrasonic sounds—distinct clicks inaudible to the human ear—when exposed to drought or physical damage. Using sensitive microphones and machine learning algorithms, the team trained AI systems to not only detect but also classify the type of stress the plant was experiencing. Tomato and tobacco plants under duress emitted ultrasonic emissions around 40 to 80 kHz, and the AI could distinguish between water stress and cutting injury with high accuracy. This study was among the first to combine bioacoustics with artificial intelligence to interpret plant communication, opening new possibilities for non-invasive crop monitoring and precision agriculture. It validated the concept that plants broadcast distress signals into their environment, and that emerging tech can now listen—and respond—on their behalf.

Climate Change and Plant Resilience

As the global climate continues to shift, the ability of plants to adapt and survive has become a critical area of research. Rising temperatures, changing precipitation patterns, and increased frequency of extreme weather events are all placing new pressures on plant life, forcing them to develop novel strategies for survival. Understanding how plants respond to these environmental changes is essential for predicting the future of ecosystems and developing effective conservation and agricultural strategies.

One of the most significant challenges posed by climate change is the increasing frequency of droughts, which can severely impact plant growth and survival. Many species have evolved mechanisms to cope with water scarcity, such as deep root systems, waxy leaf coatings, and the ability to enter dormancy during dry periods. However, as droughts become more frequent and severe, even these adaptations may not be sufficient. Scientists are studying how plants respond to prolonged water stress, looking for ways to enhance their resilience through genetic modification, selective breeding, and improved land management practices. For example, some researchers are exploring the potential of mycorrhizal fungi to help plants access deeper water sources, while others are investigating how certain plant species can be cultivated to thrive in arid conditions.

In addition to drought, rising temperatures are also affecting plant life in profound ways. Many plants have specific temperature thresholds for optimal growth, and even small increases in temperature can disrupt their biological processes. Some species are shifting their ranges to higher altitudes or latitudes in search of cooler climates, while others are struggling to keep pace with the rapid changes. This movement can have cascading effects on entire ecosystems, altering species interactions and disrupting food webs. Scientists are using satellite imagery and climate models to track these shifts, helping to identify vulnerable species and inform conservation efforts.

Another major concern is the impact of climate change on plant-pollinator relationships. Many flowering plants rely on specific pollinators—such as bees, butterflies, and birds—to reproduce, and changes in temperature and weather patterns can disrupt these delicate interactions. For instance, if a plant blooms earlier due to warmer springs, it may no longer coincide with the arrival of its primary pollinators, leading to reduced reproductive success. Similarly, changes in insect populations due to habitat loss and pesticide use can further complicate these relationships. Researchers are working to understand these dynamics and develop strategies to protect both plants and their pollinators, such as creating pollinator-friendly habitats and reducing the use of harmful chemicals.

The role of plant communication in climate adaptation is also an area of growing interest. Studies have shown that plants can share information through chemical signals and underground fungal networks, allowing them to respond collectively to environmental stressors. This interconnectedness may provide a buffer against the effects of climate change, as plants can warn each other of impending threats and coordinate their responses. Scientists are exploring how these natural communication systems can be harnessed to improve the resilience of crops and ecosystems, potentially offering new solutions for sustainable agriculture and environmental restoration.

As climate change continues to reshape the world around us, the ability of plants to adapt and survive will play a crucial role in maintaining the balance of ecosystems. By studying how plants respond to environmental changes and developing strategies to support their resilience, we can work toward a more sustainable and adaptive future. This research not only enhances our understanding of plant life but also provides valuable insights for addressing one of the most pressing challenges of our time.

The Role of Education and Awareness

As our understanding of plant communication and intelligence deepens, it becomes increasingly clear that education and awareness play a vital role in shaping public perception and fostering a more sustainable relationship with the natural world. Despite the growing body of scientific research, many people still view plants as passive entities, unaware of the intricate networks and dynamic interactions that define their existence. Raising awareness about the complexity of plant life is essential for promoting conservation efforts, encouraging responsible land use, and inspiring a new generation of scientists, farmers, and environmental advocates.

One of the most effective ways to increase public awareness is through educational initiatives that bring the science of plant communication into classrooms, museums, and community programs. Schools can incorporate lessons on plant biology, ecology, and environmental science into their curricula, helping students develop a deeper appreciation for the role plants play in sustaining life on Earth. Interactive exhibits, virtual reality experiences, and hands-on experiments can make these concepts more engaging and accessible, allowing students to explore the hidden world of plants in a meaningful way. By integrating these topics into formal education, we can cultivate a greater sense of environmental responsibility from an early age.

Beyond formal education, public outreach and media campaigns can also play a crucial role in raising awareness about plant communication. Documentaries, books, and online platforms dedicated to plant science can reach a wide audience, making complex scientific discoveries more relatable and understandable. Social media, in particular, offers a powerful tool for sharing knowledge and sparking conversations about the importance of plants in our lives. By highlighting the latest research, showcasing real-world applications, and encouraging engagement with nature, these platforms can help bridge the gap between scientific discovery and public understanding.

Community-based initiatives are another key component of education and awareness. Local gardening groups, urban greening projects, and citizen science programs provide opportunities for individuals to learn about plant life firsthand. By participating in these activities, people can gain a more direct and personal connection to the natural world, reinforcing the idea that plants are not just background elements but active participants in ecological systems. These experiences can inspire a lifelong commitment to environmental stewardship, encouraging individuals to take action in their own communities.

Educational institutions, governments, and environmental organizations must also collaborate to ensure that plant science receives the attention it deserves. Funding for research, policy support for sustainable practices, and investment in public education programs can all contribute to a more informed and engaged society. By prioritizing plant-related education and awareness, we can foster a culture that values the intricate web of life that sustains us all.

Ultimately, education and awareness are essential for shaping a future in which plants are recognized for their complexity, resilience, and significance. By promoting a deeper understanding of plant communication and intelligence, we can encourage more thoughtful and sustainable interactions with the natural world. This shift in perspective not only enriches our scientific knowledge but also empowers individuals to make informed choices that benefit both plants and people.

A Call to Action

As we continue to uncover the hidden world of plant communication, it becomes clear that this knowledge has the power to transform the way we interact with the natural world. The more we understand about how plants sense, respond to, and connect with their environment, the more equipped we are to make informed decisions that support ecological balance and sustainability. This is not just a matter of scientific curiosity—it is a call to action for individuals, communities, and societies to recognize the importance of plants and take meaningful steps toward a more harmonious relationship with the environment.

One of the most immediate ways to get involved is by supporting sustainable agricultural practices that respect the natural systems that sustain plant life. Farmers and gardeners can adopt methods that work with the existing networks of mycorrhizal fungi, promote biodiversity, and reduce reliance on synthetic inputs. Techniques such as cover cropping, composting, and reduced tillage can help maintain healthy soil ecosystems, ensuring that plants have the resources they need to thrive. By choosing locally grown, plant-based foods and supporting organic farming initiatives, consumers can also contribute to a more sustainable food system that values the health of both people and the planet.

Individuals can also make a difference by incorporating more plants into their daily lives. Whether it's planting native species in gardens, growing houseplants, or simply spending time in nature, these actions help strengthen the human-plant connection. By observing how plants respond to their surroundings, people can develop a greater appreciation for the complexity of plant life and the roles they play in maintaining ecological balance. This awareness can inspire more mindful choices, from reducing waste to supporting conservation efforts that protect endangered plant species and restore degraded landscapes.

Communities can play a vital role in promoting plant literacy and environmental stewardship. Local initiatives such as tree planting programs, urban green spaces, and educational workshops can help raise awareness about the importance of plants and their interconnected networks. Schools, libraries, and cultural institutions can also serve as hubs for learning, offering resources and programs that highlight the fascinating world of plant communication. By fostering a culture of curiosity and respect for plant life, we can cultivate a deeper understanding of the natural world and encourage more sustainable behaviors.

On a broader scale, policymakers and environmental organizations must prioritize plant science in their agendas. Supporting research into plant communication, funding conservation efforts, and implementing policies that protect natural habitats are essential steps toward a more resilient and balanced ecosystem. By recognizing the value of plant intelligence and cooperation, we can develop more effective strategies for addressing environmental challenges and ensuring the long-term health of our planet.

Ultimately, the journey of discovery into the hidden language of plants is not just a scientific endeavor—it is a shared responsibility. Each of us has the power to contribute to a more sustainable future by making conscious choices that support plant life and the ecosystems that depend on it. Whether through education, advocacy, or everyday actions, we can all play a part in nurturing the intricate web of life that sustains us all. By embracing this knowledge and taking action, we can help preserve the natural world for future generations and ensure that the wisdom of plants continues to guide us in our quest for a more sustainable and interconnected future.

Did You Know?

Plants emit high-frequency clicks under stress—tomato and tobacco plants have been recorded producing ultrasonic sounds (~65 dB at 50 kHz) when cut or dehydrated, detectable by specialized microphones.

AI is decoding VOC 'dialects'—machine learning models are now identifying species-specific volatile organic compound (VOC) signatures that vary by context, enabling prediction of plant responses to drought or pest stress.

Plants alter VOCs in polluted environments—research shows urban air pollution disrupts the chemical trails flowers emit, confusing pollinators and reducing reproductive success.

Sensor-embedded plants act as climate monitors—engineered spinach has been used to detect explosives in groundwater and wirelessly relay the data—an early example of "plant nanobionics."

Smart forests are emerging—networks of solar-powered sensors and AI-driven analysis are being deployed in conservation zones to listen for stress signals from plants, allowing preemptive wildfire and drought interventions.

Appendices

Appendix A

Glossary of Technical Terms

Agroforestry: A land management system integrating trees with crops or livestock to create a more diverse and resilient agricultural landscape.

Allelopathy: The process whereby a plant releases chemicals to inhibit the growth of competing plants in its vicinity.

Artificial Intelligence (AI): The use of machine learning algorithms to analyze large datasets of plant behavior, helping to identify patterns and predict responses to environmental conditions.

Bioacoustics: The scientific study of how plants detect and respond to sound waves and vibrations, and how these sounds may influence their growth and communication.

Bioengineered Crops: Plants genetically modified to respond more effectively to environmental stress, resist pests, and optimize resource use by enhancing their natural signaling pathways.

Calcium Ions: Signaling molecules that act as internal messengers within a plant to coordinate cellular activity in response to external stimuli.

Carbon Sequestration: The process by which healthy soils, rich in organic matter and microbial activity, store large amounts of carbon, helping to reduce greenhouse gas emissions.

Circadian Rhythm: A plant's internal biological clock that regulates daily processes such as photosynthesis and leaf movement, shaped by past environmental experiences.

Cover Cropping: An agricultural technique of planting crops to cover the soil, maintaining and enhancing underground fungal networks and improving soil health.

Cryptochromes: Specialized photoreceptor proteins in plants that sense blue and ultraviolet light, playing a key role in regulating circadian rhythms and directional growth.

Distributed Intelligence: The concept that a plant's ability to sense, learn, and adapt is spread throughout its entire structure rather than being centralized in a brain.

Ectomycorrhizae: A major type of symbiotic mycorrhizal fungi that forms a sheath around the surface of a plant's roots.

Endomycorrhizae: A major type of symbiotic mycorrhizal fungi that penetrates directly into the root cells of a host plant.

Epigenetic Modifications: Changes in gene activity that do not alter the DNA sequence itself but influence how genes are expressed, allowing a plant to "remember" past stress events.

Flavonoids: A class of signaling molecules released by plants, including through their roots, that can attract beneficial microbes like rhizobia.

Gas Chromatography–Mass Spectrometry (GC-MS): A sophisticated analytical technique used to identify and quantify the specific chemical messages (VOCs) that plants release to communicate.

Genome Editing: A technology that precisely modifies a plant's DNA to improve traits such as yield, resilience, and nutritional content.

High-Throughput Phenotyping: A technology employing drones, sensors, and imaging to rapidly analyze plant traits on a large scale.

High-Performance Liquid Chromatography (HPLC): An analytical tool used to identify the diverse range of chemical compounds present in root exudates.

Integrated Pest Management: A sustainable farming practice that uses natural predators and biological controls instead of chemical pesticides to maintain crop health.

Juglone: A specific allelopathic compound secreted by the black walnut tree that suppresses the growth of many other plants in its vicinity.

Mechanosensitive Ion Channels: Structures in plant cells believed to detect physical stimuli like touch or pressure, triggering a response by opening and initiating a biochemical reaction.

Mother Trees: Large, well-established trees that serve as central hubs in a forest's mycorrhizal network, supporting younger trees by sending them nutrients and warning signals.

Mycoremediation: The use of fungi to clean up polluted environments by breaking down or absorbing contaminants.

Mycorrhizae: Symbiotic associations between fungi and plant roots where the fungi help the plant absorb nutrients and water in exchange for carbohydrates.

Permaculture: A design philosophy for agricultural systems that emphasizes mimicking the patterns and relationships found in natural ecosystems.

Pheromones: Specific chemical signals, often composed of volatile compounds, that plants release to attract pollinators to their flowers.

Phenolic Compounds: A class of signaling molecules used by plants to communicate through the fungal network.

Phototropism: The directional growth of a plant toward or away from a light source, guided by specialized photoreceptors.

Phytochromes: Photoreceptor proteins used by plants to detect red and far-red light, influencing processes such as seed germination and leaf growth.

Plant Hormones: Compounds such as auxins and ethylene that regulate plant growth and development in response to environmental changes.

Plant Intelligence: The ability of plants to sense, adapt, communicate, and "remember" past events, demonstrating complex problem-solving abilities without a brain.

Priming: A form of adaptive memory where a plant's past exposure to a stressor, like drought, enables a quicker and more effective response to that same stressor in the future.

Pseudocopulation: A deceptive strategy used by some orchids, producing chemicals that mimic female insect pheromones to trick male insects into pollinating the flower.

Reactive Oxygen Species: Signaling molecules released internally by a plant to coordinate cellular activity and trigger responses to external stimuli.

Reduced Tillage: A farming practice that minimizes soil disturbance to preserve and enhance the underground mycorrhizal networks that support plant life.

Regenerative Agriculture: A farming approach focused on restoring soil health and increasing biodiversity by mimicking natural processes and strengthening underground ecosystems.

Rhizobia: A group of nitrogen-fixing bacteria attracted by signals from leguminous plants and colonizing their roots to provide usable nitrogen.

Root Exudates: Organic compounds released by plant roots into the soil to communicate with microbes, signal to neighboring plants, or inhibit competitors.

Symbiotic Relationship: A mutually beneficial partnership between different organisms, such as that between plants and mycorrhizal fungi.

Terpenoids: A class of signaling molecules that plants can transmit through the fungal network to communicate.

Thigmotropism: The directional growth or movement of a plant in response to physical touch, as seen in climbing vines.

Vertical Farming: An agricultural method of growing crops indoors in stacked layers, using less land and water.

Volatile Organic Compounds (VOCs): Airborne chemicals that evaporate easily and are released by plants as a form of communication to warn other plants of danger or attract pollinators.

Wood Wide Web: The term for the vast underground network of mycorrhizal fungi that connects trees and plants, facilitating the flow of nutrients and information.

Appendix B

Timeline of Important Discoveries

1794 – Joseph Priestley discovers that plants can "purify" air, laying the foundation for understanding plant functions in ecosystems.

1804 – Jean-Baptiste Lamarck proposes early ideas about plant adaptation and inheritance of acquired traits, influencing later theories on plant behavior.

1835 – Alexander von Humboldt documents the interconnectedness of plant and animal life in tropical ecosystems, highlighting ecological relationships.

1843 – First documented evidence of plant communication through chemical signaling, with observations of plants responding to environmental stress.

1862 – Charles Darwin notes the sensitivity of plant tendrils and their ability to respond to touch, suggesting a form of plant intelligence.

1880 – Charles Darwin and his son Francis publish *The Power of Movement in Plants*, detailing how plants respond to light, gravity, and touch.

1893 – German botanist Julius von Sachs publishes *Lehrbuch der Botanik*, describing the role of roots and soil in plant nutrition.

1905 – Russian scientist Ivan Michurin begins experiments on plant hybridization and adaptation, contributing to early understandings of plant resilience.

1914 – The first studies on root exudates are conducted, revealing that plants release substances into the soil to interact with microorganisms.

1920s – Early research on allelopathy is published, showing that some plants release chemicals to inhibit the growth of others.

1930s – Scientists begin to recognize the role of fungi in plant nutrition, leading to the discovery of mycorrhizal relationships.

1943 – The term "mycorrhiza" is formally introduced, marking the beginning of modern research into fungal-plant symbiosis.

1950s – Studies on plant hormones (like auxins and ethylene) reveal how plants regulate growth and respond to environmental changes.

1962 – Researchers identify volatile organic compounds (VOCs) released by plants under stress, indicating chemical communication.

1965 – The concept of "plant memory" emerges from experiments showing that plants can retain information about past stressors.

1970s – Initial experiments suggest that plants may respond to sound waves, sparking interest in bioacoustic plant research.

1975 – Scientists observe that plants can detect and respond to vibrations, further supporting the idea of mechanical sensitivity.

1980s – Research on plant defense mechanisms reveals that chemical signals are used to warn neighboring plants of threats.

1985 – A study shows that tomato plants emit VOCs when attacked by herbivores, alerting nearby plants to potential danger.

1990s – Advances in molecular biology allow scientists to identify specific genes involved in plant communication and stress responses.

1997 – Research demonstrates that plants can share resources through mycorrhizal networks, revealing cooperative behaviors among trees.

1998 – Suzanne Simard's early work on forest networks begins, setting the stage for her groundbreaking 2006 findings.

2000 – The term "plant intelligence" gains traction in scientific literature, challenging traditional views of plant life.

2001 – Experiments show that plants can respond to touch, demonstrating thigmotropism and physical sensitivity.

2004 – Researchers discover that plants can use underground fungal networks to transfer nutrients between species.

2006 – Suzanne Simard publishes key findings on "mother trees" and the role of mycorrhizal networks in forest communication.

2007 – Studies confirm that plants can detect and respond to low-frequency vibrations, suggesting a form of mechanosensitivity.

2009 – A major study reveals that plants can communicate via chemical signals to attract pollinators and deter herbivores.

2010 – Advances in bioacoustics suggest that plants may be capable of detecting and responding to sound.

2012 – Research shows that plants can "remember" past stress events, adjusting future growth and defense strategies accordingly.

2013 – Scientists discover that plants can use root exudates to signal to beneficial microbes and other plants.

2014 – Experiments demonstrate that exposure to music or sound can influence plant growth and development.

2015 – A landmark study shows that plants can "learn" and adapt to repeated environmental challenges.

2016 – Research confirms that plants can detect and respond to mechanical vibrations, such as those caused by wind or animal movement.

2017 – New studies explore the role of mycorrhizal networks in transmitting chemical signals across plant communities.

2018 – Scientists confirm that plants can detect and respond to mechanical vibrations, reinforcing the idea of plant sensitivity.

2019 – AI and machine learning are applied to analyze plant communication patterns, offering new insights into plant behavior.

2020 – Research highlights the impact of climate change on plant communication and the importance of maintaining healthy plant networks.

2021 – Scientists discover that plants can detect and respond to electrical signals, opening new avenues in plant neurobiology.

2022 – Studies explore how climate change affects plant communication, emphasizing the need for conservation and sustainable practices.

2023 – Ongoing research continues to refine our understanding of plant intelligence, communication, and ecological interactions.

Appendix C

Further Reading and Resources

Books:

The Hidden Life of Trees by Peter Wohlleben

What a Plant Knows by Daniel Chamovitz

The Botany of Desire by Michael Pollan

The Secret Life of Plants by Peter Tompkins and Christopher Bird

Websites:

Science Magazine – Plant Communication
 URL : https://www.sciencemag.org
 Description : Regularly features research on plant communication and ecological interactions.
BBC Earth – Plant Intelligence
 URL : https://www.bbc.com/earth
 Description : Articles and videos on the fascinating world of plant life.
National Geographic – Plant Communication
 URL : https://www.nationalgeographic.org
 Description : In-depth articles and multimedia content on plant behavior and adaptation.
The Mycorrhiza Information Network (MIN)
 URL : http://www.mycorrhiza.net
 Description : A comprehensive resource on mycorrhizal fungi and their role in plant health.
The University of California – Plant Communication Research
 URL : https://ucanr.edu
 Description : Research and educational materials on plant biology and ecology.

Classroom Activities

Chapter 1: Mycorrhizal Fungi: The Invisible Network

Discussion Questions:

1. The book describes the mycorrhizal network as the "Wood Wide Web". In what ways is this a good analogy for the internet we use every day? In what ways does it fall short?

2. How does the symbiotic relationship between plants and mycorrhizal fungi challenge the traditional idea that plants are isolated individuals competing for survival?

3. The text explains that older, more established trees can support younger saplings through the network. What could be the evolutionary advantage for the older tree in helping its potential future competitors?

4. If a forest's fungal network is severely damaged by human activity (like construction or certain types of farming), what are some of the long-term consequences for the health and resilience of that forest?

5. The chapter mentions that these fungal networks can connect different species of plants, like Douglas fir and paper birch. Why is it beneficial for an entire ecosystem to have different species cooperating and sharing resources?

Practical Project:

- **Root and Fungi Observation Jar:** Students can explore the hidden world of roots and fungi. Under teacher guidance, they can plant a fast-growing seed (like a bean or pea) in a clear glass jar filled with soil. One set of jars can have soil taken from a mature forest or garden (likely containing mycorrhizae), while a control set uses sterilized potting soil. Students will water the plants and keep a journal, observing the root growth against the glass over several weeks. They can sketch the root structures and, with a magnifying glass, look for the fine, web-like strands of fungal hyphae, comparing the growth between the two soil types.

Chapter 2: The Language of Smells

Discussion Questions:

1. Plants use volatile organic compounds (VOCs) to warn neighbors of threats. How is this airborne communication system both an advantage and a disadvantage compared to the underground fungal network?

2. The book gives the example of a tomato plant releasing chemicals to warn others when attacked by aphids. Why would a plant evolve a mechanism to help its neighbors rather than just focusing on its own defense?

3. Some orchids trick male insects into pollination through "pseudocopulation". Is this a form of "intelligence" or simply a highly specialized evolutionary adaptation? What is the difference?

4. The chapter discusses how plants use root exudates to both attract beneficial microbes and inhibit the growth of competitors (allelopathy). How do plants manage this complex balance of "friendly" and "hostile" signals in the soil?

5. Knowing that plants release defensive chemicals when attacked, how might this knowledge be used to develop more sustainable and natural pesticides for farming?

Practical Project:

- **"Smell of Danger" Experiment:** Students can investigate plant VOCs in a simple, safe way. With supervision, they can take fresh leaves from a highly aromatic plant (like mint, basil, or eucalyptus). One set of leaves is left untouched in a sealed bag. Another set is gently crushed or torn and placed in a separate sealed bag. After an hour, students can open both bags and compare the intensity of the smell. This demonstrates how physical damage causes the plant to release a higher concentration of VOCs as a defense mechanism.

Chapter 3: The Science of Plant Sensitivity

Discussion Questions:

1. Plants can detect light, temperature, and touch without having eyes, skin, or nerves. How does this "decentralized" sensory system challenge our definition of what it means to "sense" the world?

2. The book discusses thigmotropism, where plants like vines react to touch. Besides climbing, what other reasons might a plant have for needing to sense physical contact?

3. Research suggests plants may respond to specific sound frequencies or vibrations. If this is true, what kind of information could a plant gain from "listening" to its environment? (e.g., sound of running water, vibrations from insects).

4. If a plant can sense and react to its environment, does this imply a form of perception or awareness? Where do we draw the line between a biological reflex and perception?

5. How could understanding plant sensitivity to vibrations and sound be practically applied in agriculture or indoor gardening to improve crop health and yield?

Practical Project:

- **The Touch-Me-Not Plant Study:** Students can work with a plant known for its sensitivity, like the Mimosa pudica ("touch-me-not"). The project is to observe and document its reactions. Students can gently touch a leaf and time how long it takes to fold and how long it takes to reopen. They can then design simple experiments to test if the plant has a "memory" or gets "used to" the stimulus by touching the same leaf repeatedly at set intervals and observing if the reaction time changes.

Chapter 4: The Social Lives of Plants

Discussion Questions:

1. The chapter contrasts the cooperative behavior of "mother trees" with the intense competition plants face for resources like light and water. Are plants fundamentally cooperative or competitive, or is it more complicated than that?

2. The book suggests plants can "remember" past stressors and adjust their future responses, a process called "priming". How is this similar to and different from the way animals learn from experience?

3. If plants lack a brain, how can they exhibit behaviors that we associate with intelligence, like communication, memory, and problem-solving? What does this suggest about the nature of intelligence itself?

4. The black walnut tree uses chemical warfare (allelopathy) to eliminate competitors. Is this an example of "selfish" behavior in plants, and does applying such human terms to plants help or hinder our understanding of them?

5. What are the implications of recognizing that plants have "social lives"? How should this change the way we manage forests, parks, and even our own gardens?

Practical Project:

- **Competition for Light Study:** Students can set up a simple experiment to observe plant competition. Plant several seeds (e.g., radish or grass) in two separate pots. In one pot, the seeds are spaced far apart. In the other, they are planted very close together. Both pots are given the same amount of water and light. Students will measure and record the growth of the seedlings over several weeks, comparing the height and health of the plants in the crowded pot versus the spaced-out pot to visualize the struggle for survival and resources.

Chapter 5: Applying Plant Communication

Discussion Questions:

1. The chapter introduces regenerative agriculture, which mimics natural ecosystems. Why do you think modern, industrial agriculture moved away from these natural principles in the first place?

2. Agroforestry involves integrating trees and crops. What are some of the challenges a farmer might face when transitioning from a single-crop (monoculture) system to an agroforestry system?

3. Bioengineered crops can be designed to enhance their signaling pathways or drought tolerance. What are some of the ethical concerns or potential risks that should be considered when we start "improving" a plant's natural communication abilities?

4. The book states that sustainable farming practices can empower small-scale farmers who have limited access to expensive chemical inputs. How can supporting sustainable agriculture also address issues of social and economic inequality?

5. Choose one sustainable practice mentioned in the chapter (e.g., cover cropping, reduced tillage, composting). How could you apply a small-scale version of this principle in your own home, school, or community?

Practical Project:

- **Mini-Compost and Soil Health Test:** Students can create their own small-scale compost bottles to understand soil health. In a large plastic soda bottle with the top cut off, they will layer "green" materials (like vegetable scraps, grass clippings) and "brown" materials (like shredded paper, dry leaves). They will add a little soil and keep it moist. Over several weeks, they can observe the decomposition process. Finally, they can use their finished compost to plant seeds and compare their growth to seeds planted in soil without compost, demonstrating how restored soil fertility benefits plant life.

Chapter 6: The Philosophy of Plant Life

Discussion Questions:

1. The book asks if we should change the way we treat plants now that we know they are capable of sensing and communicating. Do you believe plants should have rights? If so, what would those rights be?

2. If a plant has "genius" or a form of intelligence, but no consciousness or ability to feel pain as animals do, how does this affect our ethical obligations toward them?

3. The text discusses the "human-nature connection" and the psychological benefits of being around plants. Why do you think humans have this innate affinity (biophilia) for the natural world?

4. How has the traditional view of plants as passive, inert resources contributed to environmental problems like deforestation and habitat destruction?

5. The chapter proposes "a new way of seeing" plants. What is one specific way you could change your own daily behavior or mindset to better reflect this new perspective?

Practical Project:

- **Plant-Centered Design Project:** This is a creative and ethical design challenge. Students are asked to redesign a common space (like their classroom, a school hallway, or a small part of the playground) from the *plant's* perspective. They must consider the plants' needs for light, water, space to communicate (root space), and protection from harm. They will create a "blueprint" or model of their design and present it to the class, explaining how their choices reflect a more respectful and ethical relationship with plant life, moving beyond seeing them as mere decoration.

Chapter 7: The Future of Plant Communication

Discussion Questions:

1. Chapter 7 discusses emerging technologies like bioacoustics and AI that help us decode the language of plants. Which of these technologies do you think holds the most promise for the future, and why?

2. Scientists are studying how plant communication can enhance resilience to climate change. What are some specific ways that a forest's "Wood Wide Web" could help it survive a prolonged drought or a new disease?

3. The chapter mentions tracking how plant species are shifting their ranges to higher altitudes in response to rising temperatures. What problems might this migration cause for the existing ecosystems in those higher-altitude areas?

4. The book issues a "Call to Action". What do you believe is the single most effective action an individual can take to support plant life and ecological balance? What about a community or a government?

5. If we could one day fully "translate" the chemical and electrical signals of plants, what is the first question you would want to "ask" a forest?

Practical Project:

- **"Future of Farming" Tech Proposal:** Students will work in groups to create a proposal for a new technology inspired by the chapter. They can choose an area like vertical farming, bioengineered crops, or AI-powered monitoring. Their task is to design a product or system, create a visual mockup (a drawing or digital slide), and write a short pitch explaining how their innovation uses plant communication principles to solve a specific problem like food security, water scarcity, or habitat restoration. This encourages creative thinking about the practical application of the book's concepts.

A Final Word

I truly appreciate your participation in this journey through this book. May your next read also be one of wonder, discovery, and limitless potential. If you enjoyed this book, please help me spread the word by:

1. Writing an honest review on Amazon
2. Telling your siblings, classmates, friends, and relatives about this book
3. Recommending it to your teacher for use in class
4. Sharing your thoughts on Plant Genius on social media

Last but not least, download a free Catalog and check out our other titles and stay tuned for new and exciting releases from Lexicon Labs. You can also sign up to our newsletter and stay informed about future releases. You will find links and signup details through my X account (LeoLexicon)

Dr. Leo Lexicon

Explore the lives of great innovators, Scientists, Leaders, Artists and Explorers

*Learn the basics of Coding and program in Python.
No prior knowledge required!*